Introducing Dewey

Introducing
Dewey

Paul Fairfield

BLOOMSBURY ACADEMIC
LONDON • NEW YORK • OXFORD • NEW DELHI • SYDNEY

BLOOMSBURY ACADEMIC
Bloomsbury Publishing Plc
50 Bedford Square, London, WC1B 3DP, UK
1385 Broadway, New York, NY 10018, USA
29 Earlsfort Terrace, Dublin 2, Ireland

BLOOMSBURY, BLOOMSBURY ACADEMIC and the Diana logo are trademarks
of Bloomsbury Publishing Plc

First published in Great Britain 2024

Cover design: Ben Anslow
Cover image: Studio portrait of American educator, philosopher, and author John
Dewey (1859–1952)
(Photo © Hulton Archive / Getty Images)

A catalogue record for this book is available from the British Library.

A catalog record for this book is available from the Library of Congress.

ISBN: HB: 978-1-3502-9783-8
PB: 978-1-3502-9784-5
ePDF: 978-1-3502-9780-7
eBook: 978-1-3502-9781-4

Typeset by Deanta Global Publishing Services, Chennai, India
Printed and bound in Great Britain

To find out more about our authors and books visit www.bloomsbury.com and
sign up for our newsletters.

For Gwyneth

Contents

1

Dewey's Context

A short list of preeminent new-world philosophers of the twentieth century would include a prominent place for John Dewey, and a plausible case can be made for this thinker as the foremost among this group. Whether we are speaking of his originality or influence, the breadth and sophistication of his work, or the sheer volume of literary output, this figure places second to none in the canon of American philosophy. His collected works published by Southern Illinois University Press amount to thirty-seven volumes, to which has been added a more recently published book long thought to have been lost and titled *Unmodern Philosophy and Modern Philosophy*.[1] A more prolific philosopher would be difficult to name, or one with a longer research career. Dewey began publishing while still in his twenties in the early 1880s and never stopped until his death at the age of ninety-two, producing in that time books and essays on everything from the theory of knowledge to ontology, moral and political philosophy, philosophy of education and religion, aesthetics and logic, and a vast output of shorter pieces and reviews for a wide array of publications both academic and popular. His professional career was spent largely at the University of Chicago from 1894 to 1904 and thereafter at Columbia until his retirement from teaching in 1930. He would never retire from writing, however, and several of his most important works would appear through the last decades of his life.

Dewey's published work was largely well received from an early point in his career, and his reputation and influence grew steadily through the early decades of the twentieth century in the several subdisciplines of philosophy to which he was making major contributions. *Introducing Dewey* may seem an odd undertaking given that for the first half of the last century no American philosopher gained a higher profile both within and without the academic world than this mild-mannered Vermonter. His renown among the professional philosophers of his day was considerable and based primarily upon such major works as *Democracy and Education* (1916), *Reconstruction in Philosophy* (1919), *The Public and Its Problems* (1927), and *The Quest for Certainty* (1929) while his reputation in the broader culture was due in the main to his work as an activist and public intellectual. For decades, no major social issue would go unremarked from the pen of John Dewey, and his involvement in organizations such as the International League for Academic Freedom, the National Association for the Advancement of Colored People, and the League for Industrial Democracy demonstrated a commitment to American national affairs that regularly took him beyond the confines of the university. As a philosopher he is perhaps best known as the youngest among the great trio of classical pragmatists that also includes Charles Sanders Peirce and William James and for his contributions to political liberalism and the philosophy of education. If Dewey's heyday may be said to encompass the first few decades of the twentieth century, his work went into something of an eclipse by mid-century for reasons that are not immediately evident. It can hardly be asserted that his work across various major branches of philosophy suffered any sort of large-scale refutation. A more plausible explanation is that by the 1930s and 1940s the emerging domination of analytic philosophy effectively squeezed out classical pragmatism along with any other tradition that had formerly found a home in departments of philosophy throughout the English-speaking world. Dewey's general approach was overtly anti-positivist and difficult to place on speaking terms with the new trend which by the middle of the century had crossed the Atlantic and gained hegemony in virtually every philosophy department in North America. Pragmatism was out, and so it remained until toward century's end when a revival of sorts began and a new generation of philosophers became reacquainted with this trio of thinkers and the larger movement to which they belonged—a process that continues through the present day.

This development has had several causes, not least of which is the sentiment among many that the movement that sidelined the classical pragmatists decades ago may have run its course. The institutional hegemony of Anglo-American analytic philosophy today has several challengers, and neopragmatism in its several forms is one of the more promising. Additionally, the publication of Dewey's complete works and voluminous correspondence has done much to revive interest in this thinker, as has an impressive body of scholarly literature on his thought, much of which is listed in the bibliography to this book.[2] Special mention should also be given to Richard Rorty, whose appreciative and frequent references to Dewey accomplished a good deal to renew interest among the analytic discontent and also a pair of books that appeared in 1991: Robert B. Westbrook's *John Dewey and American Democracy* and Jay Martin's *The Education of John Dewey: A Biography*.[3] The latter volumes shone renewed light on a thinker whom it had long been *de rigueur* to ignore, while more recent decades have witnessed a proliferation of scholarship that has brought back to the fore this major figure in American thought.

Born October 20, 1859, in Burlington, Vermont, John Dewey was the third of four sons of Lucina and Archibald Dewey, both descendants of generations of Vermont farmers. Archibald had migrated to the city where he owned and operated a grocery store and also fought for the North in the Civil War. John's evangelical Protestant upbringing and participation in the increasingly diverse civic life of this rapidly growing New England city would have a lasting formative influence on him, as would his university education first at the University of Vermont, where he graduated in 1879, and thereafter at Johns Hopkins, where he studied philosophy under the supervision of Hegelian scholar George Sylvester Morris, graduating with a doctorate in 1884. He began his academic career in the same year at the University of Michigan and would move on to Chicago a decade later, wherein Dewey and his wife Alice Chipman operated an elementary school that was established to put into practice the philosopher's ideas regarding education and psychology about which he had begun to write. A dispute over the "Laboratory School" led to Dewey's resignation from that university and subsequent move to Columbia, where he would spend the rest of his professional career. New York City would remain Dewey's home until his death on June 1, 1952, at the age of ninety-two.

A philosophical education in late-nineteenth-century America must be understood within a university context in which the theological faculty continued to exercise a fair amount of authority over philosophy as well as the institution as a whole. Dewey's mentor at the University of Vermont, H. A. P. Torrey, was a philosopher-preacher for whom the fundamental aim of a university education in philosophy was to provide intellectual support for the Protestant faith. Johns Hopkins was adopting an avowedly research orientation, which was a German import and an innovation in the new world, and it was there that Dewey undertook graduate studies and became immersed in the tradition of German idealism and its Anglo-American offshoot. Dewey was becoming especially well versed in the thought of Kant and Hegel and would remain within their general orbit in some fashion throughout his life. Having become acquainted with the St. Louis Hegelians as an undergraduate, Dewey, during his graduate studies, would develop from Morris a deep appreciation for Hegel in particular. From Hegelianism he was coming to regard all facets of human life as organically interrelated elements in which subject and object belong not to separate orders of being but to a single fabric in which any distinctions are contingent and dynamic in the way of any growing thing. A course in physiology that Dewey took as an undergraduate in Vermont also left an enduring impression on the young philosopher, in time giving rise to a biological and Darwinian conception of the human being in its multifarious interactions with the world. Indeed, Dewey would cite this course and its text, Thomas Huxley's *Lessons in Elementary Physiology*, as sparking his initial interest in philosophy. His university education also exhibited a growing interest in politics, history, and literature, among other subjects, and indeed it would become a lifelong trait of Dewey's to cultivate a broad range of interests by no means limited to the philosophical.

The philosophical landscape that Dewey encountered as a young man was dominated by a couple of movements with which he would need to come to critical terms and whose influence would never escape him. As noted, Protestant theology formed part of the ethos of American postsecondary institutions quite generally and largely accorded with the spiritual upbringing he had received as a boy, while in philosophy proper the principal movements that had achieved dominance in the universities through the better part of the nineteenth century were British empiricism and Scottish intuitionism or common-sense realism, although the latter had begun to decline by the middle part of the century. Darwinian biology would have a dramatic effect on the North American academic scene across the disciplines, and common-sense realism in particular lost its hold by century's end owing in large part to its rather static conception of the world. For an alternative, many, including the young Dewey, began looking to the German tradition and its British descendant. Post-Kantian idealism, and Hegel in particular, appealed to a growing number of American intellectuals a great many of whom by the conclusion of the Civil War were pursuing their education at German universities where they imbibed both an approach to philosophy that seemed to dovetail with the new Darwinian outlook and an approach to university education whose central focus was upon free-spirited research rather than the conservation of tradition. Dewey himself was attracted by what he viewed as a Hegelian reconciliation between subjectivity and objectivity which also cohered with the form of Christianity to which he continued to profess allegiance. James Good points out that

> [a]t the university level, German influences on American education included the seminar-style course, the lecture course, laboratories, research libraries, university presses, learned societies, and academic journals. . . . American intellectuals viewed German educational thought as a liberalizing influence on American universities. As these German concepts permeated higher education in America, a system of research universities rapidly replaced the system of denominational colleges that were designed to train ministers.[4]

The philosophical landscape would change considerably over the course of Dewey's long career, the latter decades of which saw the emergence of analytic thought which had been imported from Britain and seemed to many in the profession a more clear and rigorous approach to philosophy than both its predecessors and contemporary peers had managed. It would never find favor with Dewey himself, however. Some of his later works would express skepticism about "two contemporary schools, now exercising considerable influence, the British analytic school and the school of logical positivism, [which] suffer greatly because of their dependence upon pre-Jamesian psychology."[5] If the latter complained of the pragmatists' alleged lack of analytical rigor, Dewey's numerous criticisms of the new trend centered in the main upon analytic philosophy's arid rationalism, formalism, and narrowness. His critique of his continental European counterparts was equally and at times still more strident, his inclination being essentially to ignore continental philosophy in its entirety much after Marx, whom he held in low regard. The future of philosophy, Dewey's conviction had it, lay decisively in the new world; the old he came to regard as something of a spent force both culturally and intellectually, although it must be said that his first-hand knowledge of his European peers left much to be desired.

Dewey was no exception to the rule that philosophers have influences, and to identify his we must attend to the tradition in which he began working in the 1880s and which in some manner would remain with him throughout his life. While his positions would evolve over the decades, one does not find in Dewey's thought any sort of rupture, although many would claim to find one in the form of a turn away from the Hegelianism of his youth by the time his major works were being written, a determination that his autobiographical essay "From Absolutism to Experimentalism" in 1930 seemed to many to confirm.[6] Without going into detail here, Dewey's "turn" away from Hegel was nothing so dramatic as has often been claimed, but a relative shift from what he came to regard as an "absolutist" rendering of Hegel—or, better, of Anglo-American neo-Hegelian idealism—which he had imbibed while in his twenties toward a more sophisticated reading which was neither a radical departure nor a wholesale rejection of the German thinker, but a more satisfactory interpretation which he could reconcile with his pragmatic experimentalism.[7] British idealist T. H. Green would also exercise a profound influence on the young Dewey, as would the founders of American pragmatism, Peirce and James. The latter's contributions to both psychology and philosophy deeply affected Dewey's entire worldview, including James' "radical empiricism" which represented an important (one might say phenomenological) departure from its British antecedent. The new empiricism and psychology that James and Dewey were developing aimed to be more consistent with Darwinian biology as well as Dewey's quite sophisticated reading of Hegel. The problem both thinkers had with the older empiricism lay in the latter's model of consciousness as standing to the world from an external point of view or as worldless subjectivity confronting an "external world" as if on the near side of an ontological abyss. The empiricism that James and Dewey were formulating proffers a naturalistic and biological conception of experience in which the latter is fundamentally inseparable from the world, while any dichotomy of mind and world, self and other, is decisively rejected. The new biology was speaking of the living organism as fundamentally bound up with its environment and engaged continually in a myriad of interactions, or what Dewey would come to call "transactions," with a world that is encompassing and of a piece with the organism. James himself was no Hegelian, but Peirce was working out of an essentially post-Kantian framework as were the St. Louis Hegelians, who included William Torrey Harris and Henry Conrad Brokmeyer. It was Peirce who coined the term "pragmatism" in his essay of 1878, "How to Make Our Ideas Clear."[8] There he spoke of the "pragmatic maxim" as the hypothesis that an idea may be defined in terms of the practical effects that the idea's object may be said to have, while James would soon broaden the term (in a way of which Peirce himself decidedly disapproved) to connote a conception of knowledge and truth. Dewey would follow James in this, as in a great many ways, while his indebtedness to Peirce would be equally evident in his appropriation of the latter's model of intellectual investigation as an essentially social, cooperative, and fallibilist inquiry into a disputed matter and of truth as, in Dewey's words, "the ideal limit of indefinitely continued inquiry."[9] Knowledge and truth cannot be separated from the investigative process that pursues them, and since the process does not come to an end, we must conceive of both knowledge and truth as nothing incontrovertible but forever in the distance, as *sophia* for the Greeks was an object at most of pursuit and not possession. Indeed, it is no exaggeration that Dewey and the other pragmatists were taking up the Greek conception of the love of wisdom and in particular the practical philosophy of Aristotle which had spoken of moral knowledge as nothing absolute or separate and apart from the good, but the product of an unending back-and-forth of universality and particularity. The subtitle to James' *Pragmatism* was *A New Name for Some Old Ways of Thinking*, where the "old ways" included a fallibilism and a humility more readily associated with the Greeks than with modern epistemology.

If Dewey would remain a fundamentally empirical thinker throughout his career, it is important to note in what sense this is so. The new, radical empiricism that he and James were formulating was not a wholesale rejection of Hobbes, Locke, and Hume. Philosophy begins with experience, as the older variants of empiricism had maintained. Everything depends, however, on what is meant by experience, surely one of the most vexed concepts in modern philosophy. The earlier empiricism had been wedded from the beginning to a metaphysical materialism and by the nineteenth century to a psychology in which human thought and behavior were conceived in terms of a "reflex arc." On this essentially mechanical model, human activity, whether cognitive or physical, is the third in a three-moment experiential model, the first two of which are sensation and ideation, and where all three are regarded as discrete and sequential. An experience of attraction, for example, begins with the passive reception of sensations caused by an external source which is followed by an act of cognitive registration and finally a reaction of, in this case, movement toward the object in question. Experience is essentially reflexive, reactive, atomistic, and quasi-causal, and it was a model that seemed to accord with a metaphysical view of the world as a system of matter in motion. Dewey's rejection of the reflex arc was part of a larger move away from British empiricism and materialism, and it is here that the alliance of idealistic and Darwinian notions comes to the fore.

Experience as it is actually had by us—what phenomenologists would term "lived experience"—does not conform to the older model but, as Dewey came to view it, must be understood in the context of the living organism negotiating its way through a world to which it does not stand in opposition but in which it is wholly at home. What actually happens in human experience is of the order not of a mechanism being effected by causes but of a biological entity acting upon and being acted upon by other beings in an environment that is both natural and cultural. Experience is no simple affair of stimulus and response, where these are wholly discrete and temporally sequential. Rather, the two are bound up together in a way that eludes ready description but to which Hegel and Darwin both afford important clues. The process is dynamic, organic, and quasi-economic. Where James was especially fond of economic metaphors, Dewey preferred the biological, where we are to imagine the human being as a being in nature and culture which is constantly interacting or transacting with other organisms and with a natural environment, and which is engaged in a continuous process of solving problems of a great many kinds. A key notion here is relations; the human being finds itself a participant in what one scholar calls "a network of interconnections," where the connections themselves are organic and reciprocal, on the model of a garden:

> The crops are rooted *in* the soil, which is aerated *by* earthworms. Insects provide the means of pollination *for* the plants. Rain falls *on* them, and energy is received *from* the sun. The interconnections are real, even though traditional philosophers had failed to give them their due. William James was an important exception. He had already prepared the way by emphasizing the importance of conjunctions and prepositions in our descriptions of experience. "We ought to say a feeling of *and*, a feeling of *if*, a feeling of *but*, and a feeling of *by*, quite as readily as we say a feeling of *blue* and a feeling of *cold*."[10]

The world of our experience is not comprised of entities alone but of the relations that bind them into an intelligible and manageable world. Dewey's idealism would speak less of consciousness and self-consciousness than of experience, inquiry, and experimentation. Reflection is operationalized and naturalized, and any abstract antitheses are not natural givens but contingencies arising from our ongoing interactions with the world. This is what the St. Louis Hegelians had been emphasizing, a form of organicism that owed much to the author of the *Phenomenology of Spirit* but that also drew heavily upon Green and others in this movement in Anglo-American philosophy which encompassed everything from ontology and epistemology to social and educational theory. Organicism expressed a general view of human beings as interrelated in all aspects of their being into a unified quasi-organism to which the individual stood as cell to body or part to whole. A form of this doctrine would remain with Dewey throughout his career, while Hegel's dialectic would afford a model for his conception of experimental inquiry, and with a difference that will become apparent as we proceed. Both ideas would also inform Dewey's philosophy of education, in the background of which would always lie the German notion of *Bildung* or education as an all-around formation, acculturation, and sophistication of the person. Hegel would remain an important figure here, and the conception Dewey formulated would build upon the older notion as would the St. Louis Hegelians who were developing a broader *Bildung* conception of philosophy itself which encompassed ethics and politics no less than education. The American transcendentalists would also develop variations on this theme.

The list of Dewey's philosophical influences would include some of his teachers at the University of Vermont and Johns Hopkins, including especially the aforementioned George Sylvester Morris and H. A. P. Torrey. Noteworthy as well are G. Stanley Hall and Charles Sanders Peirce, with whom Dewey also studied. Of the latter he would write in the latter stage of his career, "C. S. Peirce is notable among writers on logical theory for his explicit recognition of the necessity of the social factor in the determination of evidence and its probative force."[11] Dewey would develop the point in some detail, but the basic notion of rational inquiry as a matter that does not proceed *more geometrico* but as an overtly social practice was a Peircean innovation, as was the attempt to center logical theory around this practice. Peirce's sense of contingency and fallibilism would remain deeply rooted in Dewey's work, as would James' psychology and modified pragmatism. Rescuing James from his critics, most especially those who were quick to dismiss the argument of his *Pragmatism* and *The Meaning of Truth*, was a frequent preoccupation of Dewey's, as was refining the argument and spelling out its far-reaching implications.

Less an influence than an affinity is identifiable between Deweyan thought in general and twentieth-century phenomenology and hermeneutics.[12] Each of these may be traced to the post-Kantian idealist tradition in which they are likewise rooted, and while the differences are many, we might speak of Dewey's pragmatic experimentalism, twentieth-century phenomenology, and philosophical hermeneutics as distinct branches on a single tree. Some such affinities are among the more central issues in contemporary philosophy and include themes of antifoundationalism, *Bildung* and practical philosophy, theory-practice reciprocity, the overcoming of dichotomies and a critique of enlightenment excesses, the mediatedness of experience, the situated self and replacing the mind-world opposition with a more dynamic and dialectical model. There is, of course, much to say on each of these themes and some others, but painting in broad strokes we may speak of Dewey and numerous of his European contemporaries—whom he unfortunately chose not to engage with and in most instances not to read—as attempting to work through the consequences of a post-Hegelian and indeed post-enlightenment philosophy. Some family resemblance is visible as well between Dewey and the American transcendentalists of the early-mid-nineteenth century. Whether we may count specific thinkers like Ralph Waldo Emerson or Henry David Thoreau as positive influences on Dewey may be debated, but something of the spirit of America as a new world and as frontier, of individual freedom and transcendence, is more than visible in Dewey's thought, if somewhat in the background. This unmistakably American thinker saw his country as having rightfully turned its back in many ways upon the old world both politically, culturally, and also philosophically. Nineteenth-century American philosophy had received its initial impetus from both Britain and continental Europe, most notably British empiricism, Scottish intuitionism, German idealism and romanticism, but in America it had all been steeped in a tradition of individual independence and nonconformity, and an ethos of frontierism and reconstruction would profoundly alter its various old-world inheritances. The concept of reconstruction became an especial favorite of Dewey's; *Reconstruction in Philosophy* is more than the title to one of this thinker's books but indicates the basic trajectory of a good part of his project as a whole. Intellectual reconstruction dovetailed with a characteristically American turn of mind toward new beginnings, which is readily seen in groups ranging from the Puritans to the founders. The pragmatic movement may well be seen as a late-nineteenth and early-twentieth-century installment of new-worldism, and this goes some way toward explaining its frosty European reception.

A couple of additional influences of which we must take note are Auguste Comte and the aforementioned Charles Darwin as well as, naturally, the classical Greeks. Comte was a positivist and Dewey decidedly was not; however, as a student, the American thinker was favorably impressed by the new science of sociology and at least some aspects of the project that sought the unification of the sciences and their application to societal affairs, albeit not along the lines Comte had envisioned. The two figures' enthusiasm for science was carried much farther by Comte than Dewey, however, as the latter never lost sight of the limits of scientific rationality even while he would remain largely optimistic about what it could achieve in the realm of social life if it could be appropriately conceptualized and applied. His intellectual borrowings from Darwin would clearly surpass his debt to Comte; Dewey could well be described as a Darwinian, or a Darwinian of a kind. A social Darwinist à la Herbert Spencer he emphatically was not, but from the outset of his career he employed a biological model that owed much to Darwin in conceptualizing the world of human experience. Darwinian biology represented for Dewey a naturalized Hegelianism wherein the interrelatedness between the organism and its world could be understood minus the accent on natural selection and the survival of the fittest for which the social Darwinists were arguing. Darwin had been neither an epistemological, an ontological, nor a political thinker, and it became Dewey's task to develop what he regarded as the implications of the biologist's viewpoint for the larger human world, and in a manner that rescued the latter from some of his purported disciples.

Dewey's debt to Plato and Aristotle is apparent in at least a few respects. While Dewey's empirical and naturalistic turn of mind owed much to Darwin, we might mention Aristotle here as well. The latter's understanding of nature and of natural change as orderly and governed by identifiable principles was echoed in Dewey's view in which, as he expressed it,

> the changes in the living thing are orderly; they are cumulative; they tend constantly in one direction; they do not, like other changes, destroy or consume, or pass fruitless into wandering flux; they realize and fulfil. Each successive stage, no matter how unlike its predecessor, preserves its net effect and also prepares the way for a fuller activity on the part of its successor. In living beings, changes do not happen as they seem to happen elsewhere, any which way; the earlier changes are regulated in view of later results.[13]

Nature is intelligible, and changes in human and other organisms are not chaotic but structured and knowable. They are bound up in a living being's purposiveness and function, albeit along more Darwinian than Aristotelian lines. The task of the scientifically minded philosopher is to comprehend this orderliness, and this is accomplished, Dewey held, by means of neither a static nor a chaotic model but one that is processual, emergent, and transactional. The tradition of practical philosophy that stems from the *Nicomachean Ethics* is also clearly discernible in Dewey's thought and not only in his ethical theory. Several of pragmatism's basic premises can be traced to this text in particular, while to Plato's *Republic* we may trace the tradition of the knower who returns to the world of practical affairs to resolve what Dewey would call "the problems of men."

Reading Plato would always be a favorite pastime of Dewey's, and while one would be hard pressed to find many Platonic doctrines at work in his thought, something of its ethos and understanding of the purpose of philosophy itself remained visible there. By the later decades of his career, Dewey would frequently lament the condition in which philosophy in the twentieth century now found itself. If, as he expressed it, "[i]t is perhaps too extreme to say that philosophy today is in a state of doldrums . . . only optimists, who at best are not numerous, would say that philosophy is making great headway at present." What had happened, as he saw it, was that the classical pursuit of wisdom had shrunk down from what Socrates had practiced in the Athenian *agora* to "a form of Busy-work for a few professionals," with an accompanying narrowing of horizon and diminution of scale.[14] The attitude of the Greek thinker had been replaced by that of the "lexicographical autocrat"—not a kind description but one that reveals much about Dewey's rather ambitious view of what philosophy can still be in the modern world, which is not fundamentally different in kind from what it had been for the Greeks.[15] The near doldrums of philosophy in his time was owing, as he saw it, to a few factors, perhaps foremost of which was the rather arid formalism or new scholasticism that had become predominant in the profession in the English-speaking world. Remarks like the following are typical of Dewey's sentiments on the topic and would find frequent expression in his later works: "One very popular view, now, in philosophical circles in our colleges and universities, is that mathematics is the branch of knowledge with which philosophy is most directly and intimately concerned, and mathematics is the science that has nothing whatsoever to do with anything that exists, either in nature or in the human mind directly. And by devoting itself to purely formal statements and formal analyses, philosophy, or philosophers, have found a way of escape and evasion from these more serious problems."[16] In a similar vein, "This splitting up of things that exist together has brought with it, among other matters, the dissevering of philosophy from human life, relieving it from concern with administration of its affairs and of responsibility for dealing with its troubles. It may seem incredible that human beings as *living* creatures should so deny themselves as alive. In and of itself it is incredible; it has to be accounted for in terms of historic-cultural conditions that made heaven, not the earth; eternity, not the temporal; the supernatural, not the natural, the ultimate worthy concern of mankind."[17] Similar remarks are found throughout Dewey's writings, and what they evince is a thinker deeply troubled by the state of philosophy in his day. Philosophy, as he saw it, had turned its back on the vital issues of the world and toward a formalism and rationalism that was inward-looking, neither inclined nor able to speak to the broader culture, and of no interest to those outside of a particular branch of the academic profession. The kind of social issues that had been regular topics of philosophical debate throughout its history had become "unphilosophical" in a general turn toward matters technical and disconnected from human life. Questions of ethics, politics, education, religion, art, and culture had been put aside in favor of arid intellectual exercises the point of which was evident to no one outside of a small group of specialists. Common sense had also fallen out of favor in the preoccupation with formal analysis for its own sake. All of this seemed to Dewey a retreat from philosophy's original and still rightful task of inquiring into the myriad issues that beset human experience in its various modes, and it was a diagnosis that became increasingly critical toward the middle of the century.

Dewey's philosophy may be understood as well in light of his ambitious and still somewhat Greek conception of the role of a philosopher in a given culture and time period. This is to serve a function that is the virtual antithesis of the academic specialist and technician but to examine "cultural problems" in a very general sense of the phrase, one that encompasses "language, religion, industry, politics, fine arts, in so far as there is a common pattern running through them, rather than as so many separate and independent things." As he would elaborate this point in 1947,

> The principal task of philosophy is to get below the turmoil that is particularly conspicuous in times of rapid cultural change, to get behind what appears on the surface, to get to the soil in which a given culture has its roots. The business of philosophy is the relation that man has to the world in which he lives, as far as both man and the world are affected by culture, which is very much more than is usually thought.[18]

He would often repeat the point that modern Western culture was experiencing an unprecedented extent and pace of change, and while in itself this was nothing to be regretted it had the potential to get out of hand if no one, whether philosophers, scientists, or anyone else who could claim real knowledge, should be capable in some fashion of getting in front of it. Much of the "turmoil" of modern life, the manifestations of which seemed to him ubiquitous, is owing to a failure of knowledge as university professors in all disciplines had become ever-more specialized and incapable of seeing any larger picture of the human world. What was needed, Dewey believed, was something of a modern counterpart to the Greek philosopher, a relative generalist who could venture into various disciplines or subdisciplines while taking special note of any given specialty's implications for some others, thus understanding some aspects of the whole in its organic interrelatedness rather than in the isolation that had become customary in his time. What he called the "mentally active scholar," of whom he was surely one, possesses a "mind [that] roams far and wide. All is grist that comes to his mill, and he does not limit his supply of grain to any one fenced-off field."[19]

It is no surprise, then, that Dewey's own writings include major contributions to most of the major subdisciplines of philosophy, where his inveterate habit was to analyze a given theme with constant reference to some of its cognates and in a style of prose that was often accessible to nonspecialists. The broad-mindedness and far-ranging curiosity for which he called he also practiced, as a quick survey of his book titles reveals. If "the great enemy" of knowledge "is scholastic specialization," what is needed is a relatively comprehensive view of the human condition both for the purpose of understanding and "in order that the current may receive a new direction."[20] The thinker strives to "get to the soil" of the culture and to attend to the roots that grow there, as the classical Greek philosophers had attempted in their time. They were philosophers not of the blackboard but of the world of human existence, inquiring with their contemporaries and predecessors into what Dewey would often call "the problems of men" in contrast to the purely technical and verbal problems that preoccupy many a philosophical specialist. "Whenever philosophy has been taken seriously," Dewey wrote, "it has always been assumed that it signified achieving a wisdom which would influence the conduct of life. Witness the fact that almost all ancient schools of philosophy were also organized ways of living, those who accepted their tenets being committed to certain distinctive modes of conduct; witness the intimate connection of philosophy with the theology of the Roman church in the Middle Ages, its frequent association with religious interests, and, at national crises, its association with political struggles."[21] Dewey would never be an opponent of philosophical theorizing, but the crucial point for him and his fellow pragmatists was that theoretical rationality is not an end in itself but belongs to the larger effort of coming to critical terms with our practices. Theory and practice form a unified structure where the latter is the alpha and omega of theory-construction and the function of the former is to provide illumination on the myriad undertakings in which human beings engage and to advance hypotheses whose orientation is toward resolving the "problematic situations" that arise in the course of practical life. The pragmatic movement in many ways may be understood as an effort to draw down to earth the speculations of philosophers and academics across the disciplines and to orient them back to the complex terrain of human experience and human problems. It was the existential vacuity and sterility of certain forms of philosophy to which Dewey took particular exception, and on grounds that extended beyond shortcomings in the arguments themselves to the issue of their relevance. Any hypothesis, Dewey and his fellow pragmatists maintained, that could not satisfy the pragmatic maxim or answer the question of the difference its being true or false makes—from the point of view of human beings encountering a problematic situation in their experience of the world—is a pseudo-problem. A speculation, be it philosophical, scientific, or what have you, that cannot find its way back to the world is a castle in the air. The posture of what he would call the pragmatic experimentalist is toward problem-solving, and where problems are not limited to the practical in a narrow sense but must arise in at least potentially real-world conditions—for someone, at some time, in some circumstances—and where this does not preclude problems of a relatively abstract kind. The pragmatic philosophers were one and all theorists, but the decisive matter was whether such theorizing was regarded as an end in itself or was instrumental in resolving real difficulties that arise in the course of human life. In this way, the pragmatist, as Dewey saw it, was following in a tradition that stemmed from Plato while the philosophies for which he had no use almost prided themselves on their disconnection from experience. Socrates was not disconnected from his fellow Athenians and the difficulties that beset their lives, and in a similar way pragmatists "may, if they feel it necessary, draw support and courage from the fact that they are following, however imperfectly, in the path initiated by the man to whom is due the very term *philosophy*."[22]

As could be said of the classical pragmatists in general, Dewey was in many ways a common-sense philosopher. His political thinking, for instance, was deeply rooted in the American liberal democratic tradition, and while he was quite capable of swimming against the current, he was inclined toward neither adopting extreme positions nor striking radical poses at any point in his career. His views on education as well, while in some ways radical, were more measured and nuanced than the progressive movement which would claim him as an influence. On the question of religion, his *A Common Faith* of 1934 strives to articulate a conception of faith that "has always been implicitly the common faith of mankind" rather than a theologically controversial position.[23] Many other examples may be found of an even-handed thinker consistently resisting extremes and often popular conceptions as well while remaining within an orbit of common sense. A dialectical thinker of a kind, his general habit was to reject both sides of a dichotomy for some higher synthesis, and without the drama that many a left Hegelian would prefer. Grand oppositions needed to be reunified, and it was the new world that afforded the conditions in which this work was likely to be accomplished. Dewey's conviction on this matter bordered on cultural nationalism; "America," he would write in 1944, "must be looked upon as either an offshoot of Europe, culturally speaking, or as a New World in other than a geographical sense," and it was the latter option that he urged.

[C]ontinental Europe in general and Germany in particular has been the home of the practices and the philosophy based on strict separation between science as technical and ever changing and morals conceived in terms of fixed, unchanging principles. If the name 'New World' applies to the American scene, it is because we have the task of bringing into cooperative union the things that the philosophy and the education to which we are being urged to return have kept divided.[24]

As for political influences, Dewey was a clear representative of an American liberalism that owed much to the founders but that had evolved by the close of the nineteenth century and the early decades of the twentieth into the "new liberalism" whose major British exponents included the aforementioned T. H. Green along with Leonard Trelawny Hobhouse and J. A. Hobson, among others. John Stuart Mill also bears mention here; Dewey's approach to moral and political philosophy was consequentialist without being utilitarian and was more inclined toward Green's organicism than the kind of individualism that Mill favored, even while something of the spirit of utilitarian liberalism that one finds in *On Liberty* may be discerned in Dewey's work as well. For all such theorists, free speech or free inquiry is the lifeblood of democracy, and if the consequences of this hypothesis for these liberal thinkers would differ, they would do so only in part. All were left-leaning liberal democrats, and in Dewey's case he may also be counted a left Hegelian in the tradition of Green. Many of Dewey's public policy positions were also contingent upon events and myriad political actors and writers among his contemporaries, to many of whom he was often responding either in books or in the numerous shorter pieces he would publish in various newspapers and periodicals.

It is unsurprising that this common-sense philosopher would expend a great deal of labor throughout his career writing and speaking as a public intellectual. A good portion of Dewey's renown in American life was owing more to his work as an activist for a wide variety of social causes than to his more scholarly efforts, activities that ranged from participation in various organizations to writing for general audiences on issues ranging from the Pullman strike of 1894 to two world wars, the New Deal, the Great Depression, academic freedom, the rights of women, and the commission to investigate Leon Trotsky over which Dewey presided, among various others. Indeed, a sizeable portion of his collected works is comprised of innumerable brief essays, reviews, and miscellany that he was forever composing for any number of outlets. As America's foremost public intellectual for half a century, there were few cultural or political issues on which Dewey would be silent.

One final note by way of introduction to this study concerns Dewey's style of writing. Many readers of this philosopher have commented upon both the ambiguity and the blandness of his prose, often to the point of exaggeration. Even those of us who find his work on balance compelling are likely to find the experience of plowing through a text like *Unmodern Philosophy and Modern Philosophy* or *Logic: The Theory of Inquiry* about as thrilling as a walk through a modern suburb. A master stylist he was not; however, a couple of comments in his defense may be in order. First, when regarded in the context of his time and place, Dewey's writings on the whole were not atypical of the philosophical prose one finds in the tradition in which he was working. He was no William James, but James himself was hardly a typical writer for his era and he also encountered no end of difficulty from critics for many an artful turn of phrase. Dewey himself would often need to clarify his friend's positions on a number of issues and defend him against often hostile critics, and in doing so would reverse James' occasional penchant for artful expression over precision. Anglo-American philosophy in Dewey's lifetime, if I may venture a generalization, was not known for being colorful and typically exhibited less of this quality than its continental European counterpart, particularly in the case of the analytic philosophy that emerged in the final phase of Dewey's career. Blandness was not unique to this writer, and nor was ambiguity. Dewey's prose could be opaque and at times obscure, but again likely no more so than the great majority of his peers and a good deal less than many of them. Some of his lengthier and more technical works, especially in his later period, do sacrifice accessibility and style for technical precision, but this is not usually counted as a failing in modern philosophy. The countless shorter pieces that he wrote for popular audiences were far more accessible, if still a tad gray. As a rule, Dewey's writing style aims for clarity and forthrightness rather than elegance, and while traces of the latter value are evident in many of his works, it was not among his major concerns.

Notes

1 All references to Dewey's work in what follows are from *The Collected Works of John Dewey, 1882-1953*, published variously between 1969 and 1991 by Southern Illinois University Press and edited by Jo Ann Boydston. They are divided into *The Early Works* (EW), *The Middle Works* (MW), and *The Later Works* (LW), and they will be cited in what follows as either EW, MW, or LW followed by the volume number and year of original publication along with the title of the relevant text. *Unmodern Philosophy and Modern Philosophy* was also published by Southern Illinois University Press in 2012.

2 John Dewey, *The Correspondence of John Dewey*, CD-ROM, general editor Larry Hickman (Charlottesville: InteLex Corporation, 1999).

3 Robert B. Westbrook, *John Dewey and American Democracy* (Ithaca: Cornell University Press, 1991). Jay Martin, *The Education of John Dewey: A Biography* (New York: Columbia University Press, 1991). Also see Richard Rorty, *Philosophy and the Mirror of Nature* (Princeton: Princeton University Press, 1981).

4 James A. Good, *A Search for Unity in Diversity: The 'Permanent Hegelian Deposit' in the Philosophy of John Dewey* (Lanham: Lexington, 2006), 62.

5 Dewey, "William James as Empiricist," LW 15 (1942), 14.

6 Dewey, "From Absolutism to Experimentalism," LW 5 (1930), 147–160.

7 For a detailed exposition of this theme, see Good's *A Search for Unity in Diversity*.

8 Charles Sanders Peirce, "How to Make Our Ideas Clear," *Popular Science Monthly*, vol. 12, 1878.

9 Dewey, "Experience, Knowledge and Value: A Rejoinder," LW 14 (1939), 56.

10 Raymond D. Boisvert, *John Dewey: Rethinking Our Time* (Albany: State University of New York Press, 1997), 21.

11 Dewey, *Logic: The Theory of Inquiry*, LW 12 (1938), 484.

12 See Paul Fairfield, ed. *John Dewey and Continental Philosophy.* (Carbondale: Southern Illinois University Press, 2010).

13 Dewey, "The Influence of Darwinism on Philosophy," MW 4 (1909), 5.

14 Dewey, "Modern Philosophy," LW 16 (1952), 411.

15 Dewey, "Half-Hearted Naturalism," LW 3 (1927), 73.

16 Dewey, "Lessons from the War—in Philosophy," LW 14 (1940), 333–4.

17 Dewey, *Knowing and the Known*, LW 16 (1949), 249.

18 Dewey, "The Future of Philosophy," LW 17 (1947), 466–7.

19 Dewey, "The Way Out of Educational Confusion," LW 6 (1931), 87.

20 Dewey, "Bankruptcy of Modern Education" and "Philosophy and Civilization," LW 3 (1927), 278, 7.

21 Dewey, *Democracy and Education*, MW 9 (1916), 334.

22 Dewey, "Philosophy's Future in Our Scientific Age: Never Was Its Role More Crucial," LW 16 (1949), 377.

23 Dewey, *A Common Faith*, LW 9 (1933–4), 58.

24 Dewey, "Challenge to Liberal Thought," LW 15 (1944), 274.

2

Post-Hegelian Idealism and the Concept of Experience

It can be said of any philosopher that their body of work must be understood within the context of a tradition and the time period in which it was written, and Dewey is no exception to the rule. As we noted in Chapter 1, Anglo-American idealism constituted a major current in the universities in which Dewey was educated and began his professional career, and its influence ran deep not only in an early phase of his work but throughout it. In his often-cited essay of 1930, "From Absolutism to Experimentalism," he acknowledged the evident fact "that acquaintance with Hegel has left a permanent deposit in my thinking," although many of his readers would long overlook this or deny it entirely, whether on account of an unfamiliarity with Hegel or positive hostility toward his work.[1] Dewey would never be an orthodox Hegelian, but the influence of the German thinker and also the nineteenth-century American Hegelian movement would be permanent indeed in his writings. James A. Good has shown in some detail "that Dewey combined a neo-humanistic reading of Hegel that the St. Louis Hegelians proffered with a historicist reading that he developed because of the influence of Darwinian biology and developments in psychology."[2] The details of Good's argument I shall not go into here, however, what I propose to set forth in this chapter are several major themes that go to the root of Dewey's philosophical outlook in general and which encompass both ontology and the theory of knowledge. It is no exaggeration to assert that neither Dewey's pragmatic experimentalism, his moral or political philosophy, his philosophy of education, art, or religion, nor his conception of logic can be understood wholly apart from an ontology which is a variation on the idealism that he imbibed at an early stage in his career and which the present chapter endeavors to outline.

In the same essay just cited, Dewey acknowledged the "enduring influence" of his doctoral supervisor at Johns Hopkins, the notable Hegelian George Sylvester Morris, while adding that

> [t]he 'eighties and 'nineties were a time of new ferment in English thought; the reaction against atomic individualism and sensationalistic empiricism was in full swing. It was the time of Thomas Hill Green, of the two Cairds [Edward and John], of [William] Wallace. . . . This movement was at the time the vital and constructive one in philosophy. Naturally its influence fell in with and reinforced that of Professor Morris.[3]

Post-Kantian and indeed post-Hegelian idealism had migrated westward and was being heavily filtered by an English-speaking movement bent on clarifying and refining the German doctrine while also reconciling it with common sense and, in Dewey's work, Darwinian biology. This long and exceedingly complex story prominently features a critique of classical British empiricism for which, as he would express it at the outset of his career,

> We are not to determine the nature of reality or of any object of philosophical inquiry by examining it as it is in itself, but only as

it is an element in our knowledge, in our experience, only as it is related to our mind, or is an 'idea.' . . . [T]he nature of all objects of philosophical inquiry is to be fixed by finding out what experience says about them.

The basic hypothesis that "nothing shall be admitted into philosophy which does not show itself in experience" would remain with Dewey in some form throughout his career, and an enormous intellectual labor would be expended working out its full significance and implications.[4] Nothing—or nothing knowable—was outside of experience, not the concepts of reason, the moral law, nor any ordered system into which we could inquire. We begin with the experience of human beings in their ordinary dealings with the world, and without "the spirit of absolutism" that Dewey attributed to Kant in particular but also to a broad range of continental rationalists and idealists. His own idealism was to be an "experimentalism" for which contingency and change are "no longer looked upon as a fall from grace, as a lapse from reality or a sign of imperfection of Being. Modern science no longer tries to find some fixed form or essence behind each process of change. Rather, the experimental method tries to break down apparent fixities and to induce changes."[5]

A new-world idealism would need to be reconciled with a more scientific and democratic spirit, and its logic would no longer be an affair of apriorism but a social undertaking whose orientation is toward resolving real-world problems. This was not a turn away from Hegel but a fundamentally Hegelian rejection of an empiricism that had spoken of unmediated sense impressions and of experience and mind itself as in any way ahistorical. Hegel's accent upon the historical and the dialectical would be preserved and reconfigured in Dewey's thought, as everything pertaining to mind and its interactions with the world would be both socialized and historicized. The dialectic would be transformed into a theory of rational investigation that is mediated by historically inherited categories as well as overtly dialogical and contingent upon incessant interactions with an environment that is both natural and cultural. Ideas mediate all facets of our experience of the world while being nothing more absolute than hypotheses which remain subject to the ongoing course of inquiry. A spirit of social reform and "left Hegelianism" would characterize Dewey's work throughout his career while again transforming this in a manner that dovetailed with American democracy. The larger picture is complex indeed, and to approach it we must place in suspension dichotomies of ideal and real, rational and empirical, phenomena and noumena, subjectivity and objectivity, and instead regard these as functional distinctions within an experiential whole. Organic metaphors would pervade the various aspects of Dewey's thought from ontology and theory of knowledge to his social and educational philosophy, and where his constant tendency was to search for unification amid the abounding variety and complexity of the world. It was neither Hegel nor idealism in general that Dewey would reject but the transcendent absolute and indeed a good part of the metaphysical and epistemological problematic of modern philosophy. "Increasingly," as Good points out, "Dewey eliminated metaphysics by explaining elements of experience as functions within a process rather than as substantial entities," and "Dewey believed he found this functionalism in Hegel."[6] All objects of knowledge are conditioned by what Dewey would term "intelligence" or by an experience that is rational and experimental and which does not stand at some remove from the world but is bound up with it in every respect.

What he would reject, albeit not root and branch, is the older British empiricism which had presupposed a number of things that Dewey would find untenable, beginning with the subject-object opposition in which the two are regarded in a basically Cartesian way as separate orders of being while the business of knowledge is to ascertain methodologically whether ideas located in minds correspond to objects of the external world. For classical empiricism, "matters of fact" are grasped by a mind that receives the various impressions of sense before setting about to arrange these into some orderly configuration. Experience is fundamentally receptive and passive and is the ultimate court of appeal on all knowledge claims that pertain to a world which is wholly apart from consciousness. Mind itself comprises discrete faculties of perception, memory, imagination, reasoning, and so on, each of which reckons with "simple ideas" which themselves are rather uncomplicated deliverances of sense and which may be variously combined and arranged. The compulsory quality of such ideas is the ground of their validity while any relations between them are not experienced but inferred. Thinking and experiencing are separate matters, and only the former is properly regarded as an activity in the form of empiricism that Dewey would abandon. Nor, in his view, are perception, reasoning, and so on separate faculties of mind or "powers in themselves, but are such only with reference to the ends to which they are put, the services which they have to perform."[7]

What Dewey was objecting to in British empiricism is not the postulate that experience is the ultimate basis of knowledge but the "stubborn particularism" that was "its outstanding trait."[8] The particularism of mental faculties and of ideas and experienced qualities failed to accord with our actual experience of the world. James' "radical empiricism" was speaking of a "stream of consciousness," and Dewey would follow him in positing a model of awareness in which relations and continuity belong immediately to our experience of the world while simple ideas are less simple and more interpretive than the older empiricism had supposed. "Perception," as he would remark at the outset of his career, "is not passive reception; it is the active outgoing construction of mind," although the distinction between reception and construction would require a great deal of elucidation.[9] The problem with empiricism was not experience itself but how this notion had been articulated in the works of Thomas Hobbes, John Locke, David Hume, and so on, and in particular the separation of thought and experience that one finds in their works. For both James and Dewey, some form of thinking or intelligence belongs to experience from the outset; reason itself is nothing extra-empirical but is a feature of our everyday perceptions and dealings with the world. Nothing about the mind is passive or wholly uncreative, acultural, or ahistorical, and if the older empiricism overlooked or denied this, then it fell to their pragmatist descendants to provide the corrective.

As Dewey saw it, the empiricists of the seventeenth and eighteenth centuries had presupposed an altogether artificial conception of experience. The "relations or dynamic continuities" that belong to human experience as it is lived received a wholly unempirical analysis as later inferences from experience rather than ingredients of it. In his words,

> The experience of a living being struggling to hold its own and make its way in an environment, physical and social, partly facilitating and partly obstructing its actions, is of necessity a matter of ties and connexions, of bearings and uses. The very point of experience . . . is that it doesn't occur in a vacuum . . . [but] is bound up with the movement of things by most intimate and pervasive bonds.[10]

Where experience had been conceptualized as in some way separate from "experienced things," Dewey would deny the separation, regarding it as a philosophical abstraction imposed upon experience rather than something found within it. The human being is in no way separate from its natural and cultural world and from the myriad things with which it is in continual interaction, while the things themselves are nothing apart from "what they are experienced *as*, or experienced *to be*," as the phenomenological movement—largely unbeknownst to Dewey—was also asserting.[11] That rationality is external to experience was a premise shared by rationalists and empiricists alike, and pragmatists would reject the premise together with any notion of consciousness as either passive, mechanistic, or unmediated; it does not originate in raw sense data to which discrete mental faculties will later set to work, nor does it stand at some remove from either experiential objects themselves or the language and culture that condition our awareness of them.

If the basic error of classical empiricism in Dewey's estimation lay with the concept of experience itself, what was needed was a new articulation of this contested term which better accorded with what he had appropriated from both Hegel's idealism and evolutionary biology, and at this point matters become complex. The notion of experience would factor prominently in Dewey's thought across a range of philosophical areas as would the word itself in a great many book and essay titles throughout the course of his career, although many of Dewey's readers have long found his meaning elusive. We shall return to this central concept in his work throughout this study, but for now let us offer a preliminary interpretation of Dewey's conception of experience as follows. Let us begin with his notion of experiential primacy, an idea that is consistent in a number of ways with the phenomenology that stemmed from the work of Edmund Husserl. The latter writer and the larger movement that he inspired had no discernible influence on either James or Dewey, but a variety of both phenomenological and pragmatic thinkers, including Dewey, were proposing that philosophical investigation begins with the "lived experience" of human beings in their everyday dealings with what

Husserl was calling a "lifeworld" and what Dewey would refer to as situations and the ordinary difficulties that confront each of us in the midst of our natural and social environment. Thinking does not take place in any experiential vacuum or realm of pure reason but in the midst of a world that is shot through with difficulties and obscurities of a great many kinds. It begins with ordinary human experience and consists essentially in a continual project of resolving the "problematic situations" with which our existence is constantly confronted. What we are not confronted with are the numerous dualities of which philosophers have spoken from the outset of the Western tradition and which continue to beguile our efforts both to understand our condition and to resolve the difficulties that arise within it. Dewey's "new philosophy of experience and knowledge . . . no longer puts experience in opposition to rational knowledge and explanation," and indeed it jettisons radical dualities in general.[12] What such dichotomies commonly amount to, on his account, are false reifications of many of the pragmatic distinctions with which our ordinary ways of thinking about the world operate, essentially transforming abstractions of our own devising into entities and then reading them back into reality. All such hypostatization involves a false imposition upon the world of categories we have created while imagining that we are merely beholding what is there, and it is a fallacy that Dewey regarded as pervasive in the history of Western philosophy. Divisions between subject and object or reason and sensation are not false when regarded as useful distinctions that arise within our experience of the world, but the fallacy is to reify the terms of such distinctions into beings that stand in an oppositional relation. If philosophy throughout its history has exhibited a tendency to become bewitched by its own abstractions, its challenge is to conceive all distinctions of this order as nothing more than hypotheses which have been useful in resolving the situations in our experience in which we are brought up short.

Experience in its "everyday untechnical meaning" is not limited to experiences of knowledge but pertains more widely to the various meanings and situations that we encounter in the course of ordinary life.[13] Against the "intellectualism" that Dewey associated with the lion's share of modern epistemology, the "things" with which our experience deals "are objects to be treated, used, acted upon and with, enjoyed and endured, even more than things to be known. There are things *had* before they are things cognized."[14] Here again, Dewey unknowingly aligned himself with phenomenology while always insisting that it is experience in this primary sense that is the starting point and the source of all philosophical problems. In arguing thus, he was rejecting what he regarded as the two principal connotations of the term experience that are found in the history of philosophy. The first conception originated with the Greeks and persisted in some form until the seventeenth century. On this view, experience encompasses those forms of knowledge that are a product of tradition and essentially amount to the accumulated learning of prior generations, whether in the form of useful information, the practical arts, or common knowledge. With the Greeks—Plato in particular—experience in this sense of the term received a primarily derogatory connotation and was contrasted with reason and knowledge which were the proper concern of philosophers. By the early modern period, empiricists would speak of experience in a manner that appeared more consistent with developments in modern science and which was bound up with the empirical method. Experience was now the foundation of knowledge, for empiricists at any rate, while the distinction with reason was categorical. In the writings of the classical empiricists, the building blocks of knowledge were experiences in the sense of simple ideas or discrete deliverances of sense which had a self-evident quality to them, as was commonly illustrated by such statements as "This is red," G. E. Moore's "Here is one hand," and similar propositions, each of which pointed to an evident fact about the external world. There was no ratiocination to speak of in experiences of this order. Rational investigation came later and consisted in so much interrogating, analyzing, synthesizing, and inferring in a manner that could always be traced back to simple ideas, the frequent refrain being that there is nothing in the mind that was not once in the senses.

For Dewey, what both of these conceptions had overlooked is the more active, creative, and experimental dimension of experience that is at the heart of his own model. As he would state in 1949, "my *philosophical* view, or theory, of experience does not include any existence beyond *the reach* of experience," however it does aim to encompass and to do justice to everything that lies within it, and what we find within it are some matters that are less rigid and more processual than we may imagine.[15] Recalling James' stream metaphor, Dewey's conception of experience importantly includes not only "things"—all those material and ideal objects which are known to scientists, mathematicians, and so on—but relations between things and the various continuities, leadings, and consummations that are also found within and that animate human experience. There is no decoupling consciousness from its objects, for all thinking and experiencing is a thinking-about-X, where X may be anything from a material object to a situation, difficulty, hypothesis, or a relation between beings. All thinking and experiencing occur within a context in which are visible all manner of connections, from causes and effects to responses, anticipations, spatial and temporal relations, and so on, on a model that is essentially organic:

> When experience is aligned with the life-process and sensations
> are seen to be points of readjustment, the alleged atomism of

sensations totally disappears. With this disappearance is abolished the need for a synthetic faculty of super-empirical reason to connect them. Philosophy is not any longer confronted with the hopeless problem of finding a way in which separate grains of sand may be woven into a strong and coherent rope—or into the illusion and pretence of one.[16]

The error of the older empiricism was to regard such connections and organization as external impositions upon experience rather than anything internal to it, whereas the actual impositions were notions of atomic sensations and acontextual perceptions which the British empiricists posited and to which nothing in our experience conforms. Indeed, our actual consciousness of the world is replete with such relations while it is the supposed dualities of reason and sense, subjectivity and objectivity, internal and external, and so on, that are artificial.

Philip W. Jackson articulates the point this way: Dewey

asks us to abandon the convention of looking upon experience as something that happens exclusively within us, that is, as an essentially psychological concept. In its place he would substitute a conception far more inclusive, one that embraces what is being experienced as well as the experiencer. Here is the way he puts it: "Instead of signifying being shut up within one's own private feelings and sensations, . . . [experience] signifies active and alert commerce with the world; at its height it signifies complete interpenetration of self and the world of objects and events" (LW 10, 25). Experience, in other words, is transactional.[17]

The concepts of transaction and experimentation are likewise vital to Dewey's theory of experience. What the older conceptions had overlooked is the sense in which human experience in general, as he put it, is "an affair of the intercourse of a living being with its physical and social environment."[18] It is neither a purely internal nor a passive matter but is "an affair primarily of doing," of taking action within an environment with a view toward bringing about some change of conditions and with an end in view.[19] It makes as much sense to characterize such experience as taking place "out there" in the midst of an ostensibly "external world" as "in here," in some mental container called consciousness or mind. Human experience is invariably in motion, transacting with an environment and with situations which themselves do not stand still but exist in a dynamic relation with the living beings within them.

The notion of transaction connotes for Dewey a reciprocity that is at the heart of his theory of experience and which was overlooked by traditional empiricism. In an early formulation of this idea, he would write:

> All contact involves two parties; all contact means exchange, and all exchange is governed by the law of reciprocity, is commercial, whether it be exchange of thought with fact, or of cotton with shoes. As in every true bargain each side gives and each gets in proportion to its giving, so in thinking. The mind must give meaning, ideas to the world that confronts it, and in return for its investment the world gives back truth and power. The due proportion of outgo and income is the problem of intelligence as of business life.[20]

Victor Kestenbaum has noted that "Dewey's phenomenological tendency is unmistakable here; intentional act and intentional object are moments of a 'single tension.'" The model is not of an encounter between alien worlds but of a tensional commerce between parties which themselves are poles of a unified dialectic. An act of perception, for instance, as the same author expresses it, "represents a 'fusion' or 'blending' of the organism's contribution to the interaction and that of the perceived object. This fusion or integration is, according to Dewey, 'internal' and 'intrinsic.'[21] The experiencer is constantly active in a process in which it is also acted upon, and any distinction between action and passion here is relative and functional. From the earliest stage of its existence, the human being does not merely suffer brute sensations but actively handles, modifies, or otherwise does something with the objects it encounters; one brings about some adjustment to an environment, whether physically or mentally, at the same time that one undergoes something that is not altogether controlled: "Experience, in other words, is a matter of *simultaneous* doings and sufferings."[22] Even our sufferings are not as passive as we might imagine, while our doings also contain an element of undergoing and passivity. Pure activity and pure passivity are equally rare or nonexistent for us, as examples of the most simple activity or brute perception illustrate. One sees a pen on the desk; this is not as uncomplicated a matter as receiving a collection of sensations but of fixing attention, distinguishing an object from its background, viewing in context, discerning a meaning, applying language, handling the object, regarding it from different angles, bringing more than one sense to bear, and so on, while an action as uncomplicated as raising one's hand amounts to an interaction of sensations, social meaning, and communication which again implicate one in a dialectic of "doings and sufferings," however rudimentary. The living organism in general not only exists in an environment but goes out to meet it, goes to work on it, brings about an adjustment within it, and adapts to it in an ongoing series of transactions, and the more complex the organism the more complex the interactions. For human beings the distinction between activity and passivity is more a question of emphasis than anything absolute, any real experience constituting some blend of elements of doing and undergoing, a simultaneous striving and suffering. We are neither captains of our fate nor puppets on strings but organisms like other organisms but for a mode of agency that is more complex and overtly experimental than other species.

What, in Dewey's estimation, the older empiricism did not overlook but did underestimate is the role and the formative influence of habit in experience. While David Hume drew attention to this theme and was certainly alive to its influence across a range of human experiences, he did not see in full the extent to which habit pre-structures the lion's share of human behavior and cognition. Experience, in Dewey's conception, is the virtual opposite of atomistic or particularistic; it occurs within a context and has a certain continuity and trajectory to it which can escape our notice. It conforms to patterns and structures that are best spoken of as habits, if by this term we intend "definite dispositions" and "an ability to use natural conditions as means to ends."[23] "All habits," he would write elsewhere,

> are demands for certain kinds of activity; and they constitute the self. In any intelligible sense of the word will, they *are* will. They form our effective desires and they furnish us with our working capacities. They rule our thoughts, determining which shall appear and be strong and which shall pass from light into obscurity. . . . They are active means, means that project themselves, energetic and dominating ways of acting.[24]

There are several points to unpack here, beginning with the notion of a disposition. What is this but a preliminary destining to our thought or action which is carried over from previous experience, an establishing of parameters for some new experience based on what we have thought and done in the past and a consequence of the direction in which our experience has already grown. They are not easily departed from as they issue in a set of definite desires impelling us this way or that without undermining our freedom to set off in a new direction should this become necessary. Habits "constitute the self" in the sense that they deliver us from "an original plasticity of our natures" and generate forms of repeated activity in terms of which the experiencer comes to be identified by oneself and others.[25] Once formed, habits press us toward continuing particular forms of experience and make it both desirable and relatively easy to act, our action consisting essentially in a carrying forward and sometimes a consummation of what has gone before. Dispositions of thought and conduct constitute the will and indeed the self, for a given habit not only "has a hold upon us" but, as Dewey pointedly expressed it, "we are the habit."[26]

Consider any experience that one would describe as routine. Whether it be relatively active or passive, of thought or of action, an experience that has become routine encounters fewer obstacles to its continuation than when it was new. Capacities have been learned, anticipations are likely more accurate, and a general accommodation between the agent and the situations it encounters make for an outlook and often a skillfulness that one who is differently habituated will lack. One who is experienced in this sense not only has undergone a similar form of experience many times before but by virtue of such routinization has developed capacities of cognition, emotion, and action that allow one the better to cope with future experiences of this kind. Any resulting action may still be difficult, but it has been rendered less so by virtue of a facility that is a consequence of repeated experience and of any learning that has attended it. So much of human experience stems from routinized habit that it is no exaggeration to describe this as a controlling factor through most of our lives. When it is departed from, habit commonly issues in a sense of disquiet which is put right by a restoration of the equilibrium that habit had made possible. It is important to note that for Dewey habit is more deeply rooted within the self than particular experiences, actions, desires, or knowledge; it is the former that affords unity to the latter by giving it a lasting set and structure, and it is a unity that is more operative than thought. A given set of actions or experiences hangs together in virtue not of any quality that is inherent to them but of a habit that underlies and unifies them while affording them a sense of meaning and purpose. To cite Kestenbaum once more,

> For Dewey, it was a "Copernican Revolution" that "we do not have to go to knowledge to obtain an exclusive hold on reality." Immediately lived meanings disclose the world and order reality: that scientific method and knowledge have no monopoly on sensibility or intelligibility is a principle of Dewey's philosophy of experience which seems to have been almost willfully ignored by his admirers and critics.[27]

Habitual and "lived meanings" produce an intelligibility that is in a sense deeper than knowledge and is its condition of possibility. Our most basic hold upon the world is operative and lived before it is cognized.

The consequences of Dewey's general view of experience for the theory of knowledge, ethics, education, religion, and aesthetics we shall examine in the following chapters, but before we turn to these, it is important to keep in mind the departure this view represents both from the older empiricism and more specifically from the concept of the "reflex arc" which enjoyed a wide currency in the early stage of Dewey's career as a philosopher and psychologist. The reflex arc hypothesis stated that the basic structure of human activity—and mental activity in particular—is causal in a rather uncomplicated, billiard-ball sense and that the entire life of the mind can be explained within a three-stage model of sensation, idea, and response, all of which were taken to be discrete cognitive events. Mental activity in general could be accounted for within a straightforward Newtonian scheme, and the simplicity of the hypothesis goes some way toward explaining its influence. Dewey would reject this scheme for a more Darwinian, biological model. Remarkably little about the human organism, in his view, can be understood within an order of strict causality, particularly when we are speaking of minds and how they comport themselves in a cultural environment. If we are speaking empirically, our experience of the world is not an affair of assembling individual and externally related sensations or of reacting to stimuli in accordance with a rule or law but something far more vital and organic. It is more like an investigation of meanings that we are already living and of situations that we find ourselves in the midst of and which are opaque and problematic. Any movement from thought to action is not a causal matter in a mechanistic sense but resembles an experiment in which an hypothesis is enacted and feedback is sought. We are to imagine a scientist in a laboratory or an organism in the wild, acting on the supposition that a given difficulty may be resolved by means of a solution that is pursued while attending to the consequences of its application, and with a view to whether our solution succeeds in its purpose or creates more problems than it solves. Our activity is not machine-like but responsive, creative, and experimental, where any distinction of stimulus and response is functional and relative within a process that is unified and organic. Stimulus and response are as poles of a dialectic in the sense that they are internally related; the former is already contained in the latter at least as a potentiality, as is the latter in the former. There is an indivisibility at work here, an ongoing interactivity between the conditions in which an idea takes form and the consequences of its application. An animal adapting to its environment and a scientist investigating a hypothesis are adjusting and coordinating their activity based upon the consequences of prior actions in a process that is contingent and ongoing. This is neither a law nor a technique but a life process in which a given experience is not an atomic stimulus but an occasion for thought and action, and where all thought and action are in service to the worldly circumstances in which we find ourselves.

The "radical empiricism" that James and Dewey were defending constitutes a major departure from the modern epistemological problematic, a major portion of which is premised upon a series of dichotomies that fail precisely on empirical (one might say phenomenological) grounds. There is no experience of a world standing on the far side of an abyss from the subject or of mind as any sort of private container whose ideas are wholly inner representations of objects that are determinate and wholly external. As Dewey would express it, "What has been completely divided in philosophical discourse into man *and* the world, inner *and* outer, self *and* not-self, subject *and* object, individual *and* social, private *and* public, etc., are in actuality parties in life-transactions. The philosophical 'problem' of how to get them together is artificial." There are circumstances in which each of these pairings comes to function as a distinction in our experience, but the error that has been made and remade is to inflate contingent and relative distinctions into grand oppositions between separate orders of being, and where the question of knowledge becomes how to gain certainty that our subjective representations correspond to objective states of affairs in the world. Whether it be Descartes' quest for a divine guarantor of the meditator's clear and distinct ideas or Hobbes' ostensibly empirical method of reckoning with simple ideas, the business of knowing does not involve leaping over a wall separating mind and world but is something more dynamic and organic. He would speak of it as a "life-process" or a "life-activity," where both terms signify not a bridging of alien worlds but a transactional adjustment that is purposive, socially cooperative, experimental, and oriented toward resolving difficulties that arise in human experience. In Dewey's words, "a life-activity is not anything going on *between* one thing, the organism, and another thing, the environment, but that, *as* life-activity, it is a simple event over and across that distinction (not to say separation). Anything that can be entitled to either of these names has first to be located and identified as it is incorporated, engrossed, in life-activity."[28] Knowledge or the search for it is not an external addition to our experience but belongs to it from the outset, as do myriad meanings that are lived before they are known. The distinction between subjective and objective again is at most relative and functional, and where any relation between the two is internal.

To speak of human beings as "in" a natural and cultural world is not akin to stating that a table is in a room. The word "in" in the latter instance is a simple matter of spatial relations within material reality whereas in the former case we are speaking of a relational concept and of the world as a field of interactions and transactions in which we are always already participating and which defines the totality of our existence. The "specific *continuity* of the surroundings [of a living being] with his own active tendencies" is fundamental and constitutive of its being.[29] The "active tendencies" of a human being are nothing external to a particular human environment but locate it in relation to a world, just as any organism in nature exhibits "active tendencies" that orient it within and toward an environment which stands to it as water to a fish. It is encompassing, continuous, and inseparable from one's being not in a merely material sense but ontologically, such that any distinction between a living being and its environment is not absolute but selective and partial. We are relational beings all the way down, existing in a place of myriad and constant interactions and transactions which are internally related to our own "active tendencies." Dewey would continually emphasize the ontological accord of the living being and its world, where the concept of interaction is suggestive not of two metaphysically separate and determinate beings coming into relation from some relation-neutral starting point but of a rhythmic unity. Nature and experience are continuous, and Dewey would attempt to spell out the implications of this thesis in a great many of his writings.

In doing so, the Hegelian "permanent deposit" in his thought would remain apparent as would the deep affinity with phenomenology of which Dewey himself was largely and unfortunately unaware.[30] While Martin Heidegger was speaking of the human being as a "being-in-the-world," Dewey too would always conceptualize human experience in its various modes—empirical, ethical, educational, aesthetic, religious, and so on—as profoundly rooted in a social and linguistic world and as existing invariably in relation to meanings that are neither mere deliverances of sense nor constructions of the subject. All experience is mediated, and it was this insight of Hegelian idealism that informed a major portion of Dewey's philosophical project. To speak of idealism here does not mean that the world is nothing but a fiction that resides in minds but that ideas mediate the totality of our knowledge and experience. Any fact or object in the world is not isolated but

> is dependent or mediated. It is not what it is by its own independent existence. Considered as such it has no meaning whatever, and hence is no possible object of intelligence. Each is what it is, because of its connection with and dependence upon others. Reasoning is the act of mind which recognizes this dependence, and develops the modes of connection.

Immediate knowledge and immediate experience do not exist; every thought and perception is dependent upon another in the sense of referring, informing, entailing, or affording its conditions of possibility. To think about X is to see it in relation and never as a bare particular, including in the case of basic perception:

The sensation which I have, the direct presentation, does not tell me that this is a book. I know that this is a book when I can refer these present sensations to my past experience and interpret them thereby. Were it not for this act of reference the sensations would have no meaning, and would not be interpreted as a book, or as anything else. All knowledge implies, in short, a going beyond what is sensuously present to its connection with something else, and it is this act of going beyond the present which constitutes the mediate factor.[31]

This hypothesis from Dewey's early period would not fundamentally change in his later writings, although the model of experimental inquiry which is the subject of our next chapter would provide it with further elaboration and refinement. The "going beyond" to which he refers here includes a number of factors, including the store of previous experiences whether individual or socially shared, a context of meaning in which "what is sensuously present" may be viewed in relation, and any "acquired habitual modes of understanding" which we have inherited from our culture.[32] To every new experience we bring a wealth of past experiences with which the meaning of the new may be grasped—again always in relational terms and never in itself. We bring as well a standpoint and a vocabulary of linguistic concepts from which the experience becomes intelligible. Concepts enable us to transfer meaning from one particular to another and so to illuminate it, while a standpoint governs the selectivity that all experience involves. It is, he would claim, "an absurdity" to see or to think from a "standpoint which is nowhere in particular and from which things are not seen at a special angle."[33] From a given perspective it becomes possible to perceive whatever object of knowledge or experience one cares to name in a particular way and to grasp its meaning within a network of relations. Dewey defined "understanding" as an act of discerning meaning, where "[t]o grasp the meaning of a thing, an event, or a situation is to see it in its *relations* to other things: to note how it operates or functions, what consequences follow from it, what causes it, what uses it can be put to." Especially important in his view is "[t]he relation of *means-consequence* [that] is the centre and heart of all understanding."[34]

Dewey would not develop these themes in the manner or to the extent of a Nietzsche, a Heidegger, or a Merleau-Ponty—an unfortunate consequence of his lack of acquaintance with the continental philosophy of his era—but he did direct our attention to the embeddedness of all cognition in language, culture, and tradition which the latter figures were thematizing in often interestingly similar ways. At the deepest levels of human thought and experience are meanings, habits, language, and symbols that constitute our historical inheritance and afford particular experiences with a trajectory which is not a subjective idiosyncrasy but draws us into a community of inquiry. The facticity of experience would be a prominent theme not only in an early phase of Dewey's career but throughout his middle and later works in which the following statements are representative:

> But man lives in a world where each occurrence is charged with echoes and reminiscences of what has gone before, where each event is a reminder of other things. Hence he lives not, like the beasts of the field, in a world of merely physical things but in a world of signs and symbols. A stone is not merely hard, a thing into which one bumps; but it is a monument of a deceased ancestor.[35]

Further,

> There is no thinking which does not present itself on a background of tradition, and tradition has an intellectual quality that differentiates it from blind custom. Traditions are ways of

interpretation and of observation, of valuation, of everything explicitly thought of. They are the circumambient atmosphere which thought must breathe; no one has ever had an idea except as he inhaled some of this atmosphere.[36]

Many similar statements may be found in his writings, and what they evince is an awareness of the extent to which human beings are rooted in a culture that without denying our freedom does set the stage on which all our thoughts and experiences are played out. The implications of this for Dewey's theory of knowledge is the topic to which we now turn.

Notes

1   Dewey, "From Absolutism to Experimentalism," LW 5 (1930), 154.

2   James A. Good, *A Search for Unity in Diversity: The 'Permanent Hegelian Deposit' in the Philosophy of John Dewey* (Lanham: Lexington, 2006), xxiii.

3   Dewey, "From Absolutism to Experimentalism," LW 5 (1930), 152.

4   Dewey, "The Psychological Standpoint," EW 1 (1886), 123–4.

5   Dewey, *Reconstruction in Philosophy*, MW 12 (1920), 136, 145.

6   Good, *A Search for Unity in Diversity*, 178.

7   Dewey, "Ethical Principles Underlying Education," EW 5 (1897), 61.

8   Dewey, "The Need for a Recovery of Philosophy," MW 10 (1917), 12.

9   Dewey, *Psychology*, EW 2 (1887), 180.

10   Dewey, "The Need for a Recovery of Philosophy," MW 10 (1917), 11.

11   Dewey, "Pure Experience and Reality: A Disclaimer," MW 4 (1907), 120.

12   Dewey, *Democracy and Education*, MW 9 (1916), 282.

13   Dewey, "Half-Hearted Naturalism," LW 3 (1927), 76.

14   Dewey, *Experience and Nature*, LW 1 (1925), 28. Throughout this book, all italics in quoted material are in the original.

15 Dewey, "Experience and Existence: A Comment," LW 16 (1949), 383.

16 Dewey, *Reconstruction in Philosophy*, MW 12 (1920), 131.

17 Philip W. Jackson, *John Dewey and the Lessons of Art* (New Haven: Yale University Press, 1998), 3.

18 Dewey, "The Need for a Recovery of Philosophy," MW 10 (1917), 6.

19 Dewey, *Reconstruction in Philosophy*, MW 12 (1920), 129.

20 Dewey, "The Scholastic and the Speculator," EW 3 (1891), 152.

21 Victor Kestenbaum, *The Phenomenological Sense of John Dewey* (Atlantic Highlands: Humanities Press, 1977), 74, 54.

22 Dewey, "The Need for a Recovery of Philosophy," MW 10 (1917), 9.

23 Dewey, *Democracy and Education*, MW 9 (1916), 51.

24 Dewey, *Human Nature and Conduct*, MW 14 (1922), 21–2.

25 Dewey, *Democracy and Education*, MW 9 (1916), 54.

26 Dewey, *Human Nature and Conduct*, MW 14 (1922), 21.

27 Kestenbaum, *The Phenomenological Sense of John Dewey*, 3.

28 Dewey, *Knowing and the Known*, LW 16 (1949), 248, 288–9.

29 Dewey, *Democracy and Education*, MW 9 (1916), 15.

30 Some of the connections between Dewey's thought and phenomenology and other aspects of continental thought are explored in my edited volume, *John Dewey and Continental Philosophy* (Carbondale: Southern Illinois University Press, 2010).

31 Dewey, *Psychology*, EW 2 (1887), 201, 192.

32 Dewey, *How We Think*, LW 8 (1933), 214–15.

33 Dewey, "Context and Thought," LW 6 (1931), 15.

34 Dewey, *How We Think*, LW 8 (1933), 225–6, 233.

35 Dewey, *Reconstruction in Philosophy*, MW 12 (1920), 80.

36 Dewey, "Context and Thought," LW 6 (1931), 12.

3

Pragmatic Experimentalism

With the possible exception of his theory of education, likely no aspect of Dewey's philosophical project has been subject to as much misinterpretation as his pragmatism. From the beginning, both the term itself and the hypotheses that it expresses have been almost willfully misunderstood in a way that might strike us as odd. The early reception of the great trio of American pragmatists—Peirce, who coined the term, James, and Dewey—on the part of Anglo-American and continental European philosophers quite generally was less critical than dismissive and gave rise to caricatures that remain unfortunately widespread. Whatever the explanation for this may be, it remains a vital task to introduce Dewey's pragmatic instrumentalism or experimentalism to a new generation of readers without the caricature, which ought at last to be relegated to the past.

Dewey's theory of knowledge is the theme of this chapter, and it is a hypothesis that emerges from the conception of experience that we discussed in a preliminary way in Chapter 2. His analyses of experience and knowledge are impossible to disentangle and carry far-reaching implications for each of the philosophical subdisciplines to which he would make major contributions. The common thread running throughout his theories of education and aesthetics, ethics and politics, and even religion is a conception of knowledge that draws in varying degrees upon empiricism, post-Hegelian idealism, Darwinian biology, as well as the pragmatism(s) of Peirce and James, and most obviously the last in this list. The latter's *Pragmatism* of 1907 and its sequel *The Meaning of Truth* published two years later set forth a theory of knowledge the main outline of which Dewey would accept while raising it to a higher order of clarity and responding to the myriad, mostly hermeneutically careless, criticisms with which James' formulation of this doctrine had been greeted. Some of these criticisms we shall encounter in what follows, but let us begin with the basic model of knowledge that each of the pragmatists was rejecting for a variety of reasons. Dewey termed this "the spectator conception of knowledge," and its hypothesis was as follows: knowing some truth about the world happens when the mind, having scrupulously followed a method of one kind or another, grasps a proposition (the only item that is capable of being either true or false, according to the correspondence theory of truth) that accurately reflects an objective state of affairs. The sentence "It is snowing outside," to take a pedestrian example, is true if it is snowing outside, and it comes to be known by attending to our senses, making sure that nothing is impairing their proper functioning and that the circumstances of our perception (proximity, perspective, lighting conditions, etc.) are adequate to the task. Knowing is a methodological enterprise, yet at bottom it is an act of spectatorship in the sense that it constitutes "a mere beholding or viewing of reality."[1] Dewey's "Copernican revolution," as he would speak of it, entailed an alteration of knowledge's center of gravity from an epistemological subject gazing upon a reality that is external and determinate in its being to the myriad relations and interactions within which subject and object alike become what they are. In Dewey's model,

Mind is no longer a spectator beholding the world from without and finding its highest satisfaction in the joy of self-sufficing contemplation. The mind is within the world as a part of the latter's own ongoing process. It is marked off as mind by the fact that wherever it is found, changes take place in a *directed* way, so that a movement in a definite one-way sense—from the doubtful and confused to the clear, resolved and settled—takes place. From knowing as an outside beholding to knowing as an active participant in the drama of an on-moving world is the historical transition whose record we have been following.[2]

Dewey was making a few points here. First, neither experience nor knowledge is "cooped up in a private consciousness" or occurs in an inner sanctum of the mind but is bound up in every instance with the world.[3] Second, whether we are speaking of simple perception or complex operations of thought, the mind is not passive but participates in a process that is again one with reality. Third, the fundamental trajectory of the knowing act is from the problematic toward the resolved, and where the latter does not constitute certainty. Knowledge in every case is inquiry, hence a process and an activity that in principle is unending and leads us invariably toward further investigation.

The spectator theory is deeply rooted within modern epistemology and has long worked with notions of sense data, simple ideas, and representations which are conceptualized as so many givens which consciousness becomes aware of without entering into any creative activity, or not in the beginning. On this view, the human being's primordial mode of relating to the world is through knowledge, and where mind suffers countless deliverances of sense before going to work arranging, synthesizing, and variably reckoning with these basic experiential elements or on some accounts analyzing innate ideas. For Dewey, the basic problem with this view is that it represents a distortion of how we actually experience and relate to the world, which is immediately active and transactional rather than passive. It is better to speak of the immediate content of experience as meaningful situations and activities occurring within a context of practical life rather than as an encounter with raw givens. As he would write, "The history of the theory of knowledge or epistemology would have been very different if instead of the word 'data' or 'givens,' it had happened to start with calling the qualities in question 'takens.'" Any object of experience that we care to name has been taken, selected, and interpreted with respect to its quality or meaning before it is known in a sense of explicit cognition, and it is taken, he adds, "for a purpose:—that, namely, of affording signs or evidence to define and locate a problem, and thus give a clew to its resolution."[4] Accomplishing purposes, acting in the pursuit of ends, making things, and responding to situations are not secondary to knowledge but have an experiential primacy which had been overlooked by epistemological accounts that separated knowledge from action, mind from world, and theory from practice. The fundamental mistake of such theories, for Dewey, is the idea that

> knowing simply reveals a nature which Reality already has, not affecting or transforming or farther determining it in any way. The determinate nature of reality does *not* subsist 'outside' or 'beyond' the process of knowing it, and all our knowing is a mode of action in which the known reality gains more specifically determined character—this is an Idealism which is experimental, not merely epistemological.[5]

A pragmatic conception of knowledge replaces such dichotomies with the premise that "there is no such thing as genuine knowledge and fruitful understanding except as the offspring of *doing*."[6] We are actors before we are knowers, and our myriad activities are characterized by a contingency and a dynamism that an epistemology-centered philosophy had failed to see. At the most fundamental level of analysis, knowers are not spectators but participants in whatever it is they would know, and typically in a manner that eludes our awareness. Consciousness is constantly engaged in the activity of understanding the particular things it encounters in terms of what they do and what can be done with them. Any passivity here, such as in a case of elementary perception, is less passive than we might imagine but is an active undergoing and receptivity which is preparatory for what follows. The known object is not antecedently determinate and fully constituted in its being but is, as Dewey put it, "eventual; that is, it is an outcome of directed experimental operations, instead of something in sufficient existence before the act of knowing." Mind goes to work on its object from the outset, and in a sense not of constructing it but experimenting with it, turning it toward a purpose, finding out what it is good for, interrogating it and forming hypotheses about its nature, constitution, meaning, history, value, and so on. Dewey would formulate and reformulate the point throughout his works that we must replace the opposition between knowledge and action with a view "that installs doing as the heart of knowing." To know the truth about any given things or phenomena is not to behold them as "objects fixed in themselves" but to do something with them in such a way that "they become ever richer and fuller of meanings."[7] It is to engage in an action that is an interaction with an object that itself is not wholly separate in its being from the activity of the knower.

Knowing and the Known is the title of the last book that Dewey (with Arthur Bentley) would publish in his lifetime as well as an ontologically inseparable pairing or "twin aspects of common fact."[8] At the center of human experience are meanings the intelligibility of which is not limited to knowledge. What Dewey called our "hold on reality" is not always one of knowledge; rather, the meanings upon which our experience operates may be variously cognized or in a more immediate sense "lived" or "had."[9] An experience of meaning is always transactional, but it is not always intellectual. It involves an interchange with the world which is bound up in action no less than intellection, while intellection itself should not be understood as "a grasp or beholding of reality without anything being done to modify its antecedent state."[10] The knower modifies—interacts with, acts upon, interrogates, analyzes, or otherwise goes to work on—the known without constituting or constructing it in the sense of the stronger forms of idealism.

A major part of the work of which we are speaking, and by far the one that would occupy Dewey the most throughout his career, falls under the general heading of "inquiry," of which we shall have more to say in the following. What he would often call the "intelligent" dimension of experience crucially bears upon an investigative and experimental inquiry for which his preferred model would always be science. To some of his critics, many of whom appear not to have taken the trouble to read his texts with appropriate care, Dewey and other pragmatists seemed to be endorsing a positivism or scientism for which "science," whatever exactly this word is taken to mean, is the uniquely and supremely authoritative form of knowledge and indeed its only form, all other candidates for knowledge being relegated to opinion, superstition, and other epistemically dubious values. All knowledge, scientism declares, is scientific knowledge, and a selective to the point of cherry-picking method of reading Dewey's texts may bear out an interpretation in which he appears to be endorsing some version of this hypothesis, to wit: "*Scientific inquiry has been the chief instrumentality in bringing man from barbarism to civilization, from darkness to light, while it has incurred, at every step, determined opposition from the powers of ignorance, misunderstanding, and jealousy.*"[11] Dewey would sometimes speak rather casually of science or "the scientific habit of mind" in ways of which a positivist might approve, it is true.[12] Less casual moments, however—which far outnumber such statements and far exceed them in analytical clarity—find Dewey explicitly rejecting scientism and positivism for a view in which science, in the specific sense that he describes it, is an "intensified form" of a more general method of inquiry. Pragmatic experimentalism, as he would clarify this point, "would be misinterpreted if it were taken to mean that science is the only valid kind of knowledge; it is just an intensified form of knowing in which are written large the essential characters of any knowing."[13] "Any knowing" involves an application of "intelligence," to use his rather woolly term, and intelligence is a method the clearest and most elegantly elaborated example of which is scientific experimentation, however this should not give rise to "a possible misunderstanding": "What is needed is not the carrying over of procedures that have approved themselves in physical science, but *new* methods as adapted to *human* issues and problems, as methods already in scientific use have shown themselves to be in physical subjectmatter."[14] The method of natural science should not be imported into the social sciences and humanities on the premise that this method gives privileged access to the truth across all regions of human experience or affords a certainty that might one day bring the course of inquiry to an end. While he acknowledged the "simple fact . . . that we are living in an age of applied science" in the sense that "[i]t is impossible to escape the influence, direct and indirect, of the applications" of the sciences both natural and social, Dewey consistently voiced an opposition to scientism in the sense of an idolatry of a single type of knowledge or the reduction of all rationality to the method of physics.[15] The scientific method is an example of experimental intelligence which exhibits a precision, an elaborateness, and an apparatus which are notably impressive in their achievements and not mirrored in other areas of knowledge, but it is neither capable of producing a certainty that could in principle bring all inquiry to an end nor a royal road to truth. Rational inquiry does exhibit a general pattern, but it is nothing as specific as the positivist would wish. Its basic contours Dewey would make repeated efforts to conceptualize, but what is to be noted about it is its contingency, flexibility, open-endedness, adaptiveness to the various disciplines, and the uncertainty of its conclusions. It is a method at the same time that it is a social enterprise and inseparable from the actions and purposes that knowers bring to bear.

For all the praise of science that one finds in Dewey's writings, he used the term in a very general sense to connote "that knowledge which is the outcome of methods of observation, reflection, and testing which are deliberately adopted to secure a settled, assured subject matter," rather than "a kind of self-enclosed entity and end in itself, a new theology of self-sufficient authoritatively revealed inherent and absolute Truth."[16] Scientism, as Dewey saw it, is a modern manifestation of a phenomenon frequently visible in the history of Western thought which is to claim for a given system of ideas an incontrovertibility that is false and removed from the difficulty and the general tumult of life. It is dogmatic in a manner reminiscent of "the old scholastic logic" in which thinking is properly conducted in a realm of pure reason and on the basis of "methods which leave out (or abstract from) the material of fact, and which have no aim except non-contradiction of their own premises—self-consistency."[17] No ideas are above the order of justification and critique; nothing is to be accepted unquestioningly, as ideas of all kinds are to be treated as hypotheses which must be inquired into with an experimental turn of mind which foreswears all self-certainty. The most hard-headed rationalist never succeeded in thinking in a vacuum but only out there in the midst of a world of difficulties and practical life, looking for reasons and arguments that are nothing as pristine as they may have wished. A thinking that pretends to such purity ends up "a show of elaborate terminology, a hair-splitting logic, and a fictitious devotion to the mere external forms of comprehensive and minute demonstration." A good deal of scholastic thought, he believed, fits this description, while among his contemporaries he would mention the philosophy of Bertrand Russell as an example of a modern system that "smacks of authoritarianism appropriate to an aristocracy."[18] These are harsh words by Dewey's rather gentle standard, and the sentiment that underlies them is that philosophy dies in formalism, pedantry, acontextuality, and an intellectualism that is inward-looking and divorced from life.

The attitude of the philosopher is properly one of experimentation, flexibility, and risk. It is that of the speculator who, without abandoning reason, ventures hypotheses with some boldness and is not so anxious about committing errors that one ends up venturing and resolving nothing. The epistemological attitude that would have one propose nothing that does not meet a standard of absolute certainty failed to generate the kind of knowledge for which the early rationalists and empiricists hoped but stops thinking in its tracks. It is an attitude grounded in a love less of knowledge than of security and in an aversion to the discomfort that attends uncertainty. The speculator is a problem-solver and an adventurer in the world of ideas, and it is such characters who bring about whatever advances are to be found in intellectual history. "Every judgment a man passes on life is perforce, his 'I bet,' his speculation," he would write in an early essay, and it is a point he would often have occasion to repeat.[19] A philosophy that regards ideas in their bearing upon human conduct and the problems that beset them is, for Dewey, the only kind of philosophy that is worth pursuing, and it calls for a boldness of mind which he saw as at odds with the prevailing temper of the intellectual culture of the twentieth century. *The Quest for Certainty*, as he would argue in his book of that title from 1929, does not generate certainty but pedantry and false intellectual comfort. The orientation of the thinker ought not be toward this but toward the bearing of concepts, principles, and hypotheses for human experience. The meaning and theoretical import of an idea consist in its relations both with other ideas and with the world of human practices about which intellectual activity in general is properly concerned—not in the pedestrian sense that all thought must endeavor in some way to build a better mousetrap but that any rational endeavor that is unable to find its way back, however indirectly, to the difficulties of life is idle. An enormous expenditure of intellectual capital, he lamented, had been brought about by modern forms of scholasticism which saw academics retreating into a cloister, addressing a small audience of fellow specialists, and exhibiting no sense of responsibility to the society of which they are a part.

Philosophy must serve life—again not in the crude connotation that would become a caricature of pragmatism generally but in the sense that its alpha and omega is the general domain of human practices and experience. Theoretical reflection in any field ought not be for theory's sake but for the sake of resolving whatever problems arise within the field, and the more abstract disciplines are not exceptions. Whether we are speaking of philosophy, the sciences, or any other field of knowledge, when it is asserted that there is a problem regarding X, our first task is not to rush toward a solution but to linger over the problem itself. Is the asserted problem genuine, and if so then on what basis? Intellectual problems do not fall from the sky but, when they are worth pursuing, have a basis in what Dewey termed a "problematic situation" which arises invariably within some human being's experience of the world. By "problematic" he intended a situation that is indeterminate, "confusing, perplexing, disturbed, unsettled, indecisive," or one that "jars, hitches, breaks, blocks" the expected or usual course of experience.[20] Something happens that is anomalous, surprising, vague, or frustrating, and the task of thinking at the outset is to investigate the source or nature of the difficulty. Here what is needed is to develop "a sense of the problem" that we are considering or some preliminary take on what is happening and its possible meaning.[21] Before searching for a solution we must get a preliminary grasp of what the difficulty is and its basic contours. Such "reflective thinking," as he stated, "starts from the presence of a problem, and . . . its first business is to become clear as to what the problem is and why it is a problem."[22] One factor that looms large at this preliminary stage of inquiry is the ambiguity that belongs not only to our thinking about a given situation but to the situation itself and any meaning that is attributable to it. Situations and meanings are more than occasionally indefinite, and inquiry is doomed from the outset when we ask the wrong question or operate with a too vague or distorted estimation of the difficulty. Our initial reading of a situation affords inquiry with a preliminary trajectory, and when the trajectory—which is likely to be a question—is correct the resolution of the original difficulty is often not far to seek. The situation or meaning is questionable, but everything depends on which question we formulate and the way we go about pursuing it.

We arrive now at the heart of Dewey's pragmatic experimentalism, or what he would often refer to as "the method of intelligence." After a "felt difficulty" gives rise to a given line of investigation, we settle upon a provisional definition of the problem and go in search of a hypothesis that could resolve the difficulty and answer the question with which we began. The mode of research that comes into play here is at once empirical, informational, and imaginative in that we are fashioning a hypothesis on the basis of whatever information is to be had on our problem and imagining what future experiences we can expect should the hypothesis turn out to be correct.

Imagining here is a creative anticipation or a "dramatic rehearsal" of what is likely to follow from the working theory we are examining, paying special attention to any experiential consequences we can foresee. Let us take an example from everyday life. On an ordinary afternoon we are startled by a noise coming from outside the house in which we are sitting. The noise suggests chickens cackling in distress, whereupon we formulate the hypothesis that a fox which our neighbor had warned us about the previous day may be attempting to make a meal out of one of our hens. Instantly we call the dog and run outside, hockey stick in hand, ready to do battle with the unwelcome visitor. The hypothesis in this scenario is that a fox is threatening our chickens and the noise was the latter's cry of distress. Testing our theory amounts to anticipating that when we run outside we can expect to see a fox in the yard, quite possibly with a chicken in its mouth and making haste to flee before encountering the dog or the hockey stick. If our expectation turns out to be confirmed by the evidence of our senses, the hypothesis becomes true and an indeterminate situation has been transformed into a determinate one. In this instance the problematic situation that occasioned the inquiry was the chickens' plaintive cackle; our sense of the problem quickly generated the question about the fox, while the hypothesis or theory that the fox was threatening the chickens was investigated posthaste and quickly confirmed by our sight of the predator. Once a hypothesis is formed, our course of inquiry enjoins us to go in search of reasons that may confirm or disconfirm it, which importantly include particular future experiences we can expect. Once confirmed by the ensuing sight of the fox, we have good evidence to support the hypothesis and the inference is now warranted. Had our anticipations been disconfirmed, let us say by the sight of a neighbor's child bothering our chickens, the hypothesis is refuted and a new one replaces it.

What a scientist achieves in the laboratory or a historian in investigating their sources and evidence differs from our example not in kind but in degree of difficulty and sophistication. The method of experimental inquiry is one and proceeds in the following stages: the occurrence of a problematic situation; a preliminary interpretation of the difficulty; the formation of a hypothesis which is a possible explanation of and solution to the problem; testing the hypothesis by means of a search for information, reasons, and feedback between anticipated and actual experiences; further testing in the form of coherence with our existing knowledge and with the experiences of a larger community of inquirers; and the restoration of equilibrium which the original situation had disturbed. The latter stages of testing some new idea against a more settled system of beliefs and also bringing it into conversation with other competent inquirers are both of paramount importance. To say that thinking employs a method entails neither that we are proceeding *more geometrico* nor that we are working in a vacuum of context, worldview, or culture. Coherence and publicity are likewise indispensable conditions of any inquiry that purports to be rational, as our rationality itself is not separate from our sociability and from the constant practice of organizing our beliefs into some larger schema which is free of the sort of contradictions with which it is impossible to live.

Dewey would define inquiry so conceived as "the actual transition from the problematic to the secure, as far as that is intentionally guided," adding "Anything that may be called knowledge, or a known object, marks a question answered, a difficulty disposed of, a confusion cleared up, an inconsistency reduced to coherence, a perplexity mastered."[23] Other texts would find him varying his definition slightly. Hence, *"Inquiry is the controlled or directed transformation of an indeterminate situation into one that is so determinate in its constituent distinctions and relations as to convert the elements of the original situation into a unified whole.*"[24] Again, thinking "is accordingly defined as *that operation in which present facts suggest other facts (or truths) in such a way as to induce belief in what is suggested on the ground of real relation in the things themselves*, a relation between what suggests and what is suggested." What he would often term "reflective thinking" "involves (1) a state of doubt, hesitation, perplexity, mental difficulty, in which thinking originates, and (2) an act of searching, hunting, inquiring, to find material that will resolve the doubt, settle and dispose of the perplexity."[25] Reflection is an unhurried consideration of the grounds for a given belief, a search for reasons, as well as an attempt "to extract the net meanings which are the capital stock for intelligent dealing with further experiences. It is the heart of intellectual organization and of the disciplined mind."[26] Extracting meanings and weighing reasons demand of the mind a patient contemplation that seeks to understand a given object or theme in a manner that is often more profound than the informational and that is at once solution-oriented and creative. We are transforming the situation before us from relative incoherence to coherence and answering a question that will often be multidimensional in its implications for the ongoing course of thought. To grasp meaning is to understand in a sense of the word that is necessarily social and cooperative and that encompasses "two modes of understanding" which are "*to be acquainted with* and *to know of or about*" a given object.[27] Acquaintance knowledge is less (or perhaps not) propositional than knowledge about states of affairs and involves an understanding of meaning that more closely approximates wisdom than information. Both modes of thought crucially involve a search for coherence and clarity that does not occur in the privacy of the individual consciousness alone but is a social activity in which a conversational community seeks to transform "lived" into known meanings and inchoate into determinate experiences.

We turn now to the vexed question of the concept of truth in Dewey's formulation of pragmatism, and on this topic perhaps more than any other the misconceptions and dismissals that greeted his work and that of his fellow pragmatists no less must be cleared away before looking more carefully at what his theory of truth proposes. The caricature once again would have us conceive of the pragmatic notion of truth as a rather crude epistemological utilitarianism; truth, on a standard misreading, is a property of statements that "work," to use James' term but not in James' sense, that is, in a connotation of what satisfies the believer or brings the believer into whatever intellectual or emotional condition into which they wish to be delivered. What works is what accomplishes an aim that is often personal entirely aside from its justificatory rationale, or the rationale itself lies in the psychological comfort it allows us to feel. Truth on this view is a rough synonym for wishful thinking, and it is about as far from Dewey's (and James' and the other pragmatists') position as it is possible to get. The caricature was largely based on a less than careful reading of a handful of less than careful statements in James' *Pragmatism*, to wit truth is "only the expedient in the way of our thinking" or "the name of whatever proves itself to be good in the way of belief." In more sober moments, James emphasized that the "cash value" of a belief, in which its truth consists, is to be understood strictly "in experiential terms" or with respect to its phenomenological verifiability: "*True ideas are those that we can assimilate,validate, corroborate, and verify. False ideas are those that we cannot.* That is the practical difference it makes to us to have true ideas; that, therefore, is the meaning of truth, for it is all that truth is known-as."[28] A belief passes for true for the reason that it produces experiential coherence within a community of inquirers and not on the grounds that it produces some kind of personal gain for the self. As James expressed it, it is "the circumpressure of experience itself" that is "the only *real* guarantee we have against licentious thinking."[29]

James' clarifications did little to defeat the caricature, however, and it was left to Dewey to defend his friend and colleague against the critics while advancing his own formulation of the pragmatic conception of truth. "Too often," as he would state,

> when truth has been thought of as satisfaction, it has been thought of as merely emotional satisfaction, a private comfort, a meeting of purely personal need. But the satisfaction in question means a satisfaction of the needs and conditions of the problem out of which the idea, the purpose and method of action, arises. . . . Again when truth is defined as utility, it is often thought to mean utility for some purely personal end, some profit upon which a particular individual has set his heart. . . . As a matter of fact, truth as utility means service in making just that contribution to reorganization in experience that the idea or theory claims to be able to make. The usefulness of a road is not measured by the degree in which it lends itself to the purposes of a highwayman. It is measured by whether it actually functions *as* a road, as a means of easy and effective public transportation and communication. And so with the serviceableness of an idea or hypothesis as a measure of its truth.[30]

The satisfactoriness of a simple empirical statement, for instance, consists in its capacity to account for present perceptions, predict future experiences, and cohere with other relevant beliefs. The good promoted by the belief consists not in any extraneous emotional satisfaction on the part of the believer but in its ability to account coherently for all the relevant phenomena. The "problem" resolved by a true belief, Dewey repeatedly asserted, is solely that which originally occasioned a given course of inquiry.

Whenever Dewey spoke of truth, knowledge, or reason it was in terms that sought to highlight their operational and processual nature and to avoid hypostatization. What must always be kept in view is the practice of inquiring into problematic situations far more than any reified outcome, and when we do turn to the outcome it is the contingency of truth and its inseparability from the practice that generates it that should be accentuated. With this in mind, he would in the later portion of his career introduce the somewhat inelegant phrase "warranted assertibility" as a replacement for both truth and knowledge, the latter terms by his estimation being so deeply rooted in the problematic of modern foundationalist epistemology as to be unsalvageable. "Warranted assertibility" has the advantage of being conceptualizable in terms of intellectual procedures more than the outcome of such operations and is thus less likely to be reified, be it as "correspondence" or any other theory that insists on defining truth or knowledge from the outset as any kind of thing, such as a relation of objective mirroring between a statement and a fact. Truth is not a possessable object but a name for a kind of provisional consensus and resting place in the ongoing social practice of intellectual investigation. It designates those assertions that have been found by some body of competent inquirers to provide for the satisfactory determination of particular indeterminate situations, and neither for all time nor with the kind of certainty that rationalists and empiricists had promised. An hypothesis is warranted when a rationale has been produced on its behalf that has managed to resolve a given difficulty while ensuring coherence across a larger set of experiences and ideas and while creating a working consensus among competent inquirers. The product or outcome of any intellectual inquiry, Dewey would always insist, must not be transformed from an ongoing operational activity into any sort of thingly being, as has long been the tendency of philosophers and others whose zeal for certainty has often led them to become dogmatic about a decidedly contingent practice. Ideas, hypotheses, meanings, and principles are never more than tools of inquiry, and tools are judged by their capacity to perform a particular range of tasks. Knowledge, accordingly, "can only be a generalization of the properties discovered to belong to conclusions which are outcomes of inquiry. Knowledge, as an abstract term, is a name for the product of competent inquiries," and is not a representation of an ostensibly objective state of affairs.[31] It is neither fully objective nor fully subjective, as the dichotomy itself is false.

That we require a new way to speak about meaning, knowledge, and truth is what the pragmatists were proposing, albeit not in one voice. As we have noted, Charles Sanders Peirce introduced the term "pragmatism" in 1878 while limiting it to a theory of meaning: the meaning of any idea is definable in terms of the practical consequences that the idea's object may be said to have. While the term was Peirce's, the basic hypothesis was variously defended by T. H. Green, Oliver Wendell Holmes Jr., and William James, among others, and the latter thinker would expand its reach considerably from a theory of meaning to a theory of knowledge and truth, most notably in his twin monographs *Pragmatism: A New Name for Some Old Ways of Thinking* of 1907 and *The Meaning of Truth* of 1909. It would take us far afield to document the large disagreements that existed within the original group of pragmatists, particularly once we add Dewey's name to the list, so let us content ourselves with the latter's usage of this controversial term.[32] From the outset of his career, Dewey was borrowing heavily from both Peirce and (especially) James, and this included the term "pragmatism" while his ambivalence about the word itself became an outright rejection in later years. Dewey's mid-career writings would find him remarking, "Pragmatism, . . . which personally I should, for reasons which I shall not go into, prefer to call Instrumentalism," but also: "The theory of the method of knowing which is advanced in these pages may be termed pragmatic. Its essential feature is to maintain the continuity of knowing with an activity which purposely modifies the environment. It holds that knowledge in its strict sense . . . consists of our intellectual resources—of all the habits that render our action intelligent."[33] The "reasons which I shall not go into" for substituting "instrumentalism" for the older, rather embattled term evidently pertained to his mounting frustration with critiques of pragmatism (particularly of James) for which James and Dewey had both made repeated efforts to provide clarifications which seemed to be falling on deaf ears. By 1938 he would write, "Perhaps the word [pragmatism] lends itself to misconception. At all events, so much misunderstanding and relatively futile controversy have gathered about the word that it seemed advisable to avoid its use," while he would continue to maintain that "the proper interpretation of 'pragmatic' [refers to] . . . the function of consequences as necessary tests of the validity of propositions, *provided* these consequences are operationally instituted and are such as to resolve the specific problem evoking the operations."[34] This rather important proviso, which Dewey would often have occasion to repeat, fell on many a deaf ear down through the present day, and prompted him to opt variously for "instrumentalism" and "experimentalism," terms that seemed to encapsulate the pragmatic idea without the baggage.

The idea itself broadly conceived sought to replace received conceptions of meaning, theory, truth, and knowledge which had often tended toward the hubristic with more phenomenologically adequate and down-to-earth formulations. It sought as well to reject many of the tired dichotomies which are so deeply rooted in philosophy and to replace them with what are often working distinctions. Theory and practice is an especially important example of a distinction that is as old as philosophy itself and that may be retained provided that it is regarded no longer as a grand opposition but as a distinction much smaller in scale and hemmed about with contingency. This opposition he regarded as a holdover from Greek times and its division between an aristocratic class that prided itself on cultural and intellectual accomplishment and a subject class whose business it was to look after the pragmatic and material dimension of life. This division in ancient political economy became wedded to philosophy from the beginning and persisted into the modern era, where it assumed multiple forms in multiple disciplines. Dewey's aim was not to denigrate theoretical reason but to bring it back into relation with human practices in a way that is neither oppositional nor hierarchical but dialectical. Theory does not lord over practice but arises from and also returns to it, as his own theory of experimentalism takes the existing practice of "how we think"—the title of his book of 1910 and substantially revised in 1933—and raises it to a higher order of sophistication, not for theory's sake but to enable us to get a better handle on the practice itself. In a similar way his philosophy of education would not speculate in a reflective vacuum about what education should be but begin with a description of what learning already is and on that basis inquire into how this might be carried out more effectively. In an experimentalist schema, knowing and doing are conceived as a unified system while all that falls under the general heading of knowledge has the status of tools, the value of which is measured by their capacity to work in designated ways. "Pure reason" and theory for theory's sake are distortions of concepts that are indispensable, provided they keep their feet on the ground and are analyzed as "bases of actions" rather than "finalities."[35] The whole business of advancing and justifying assertions is analyzable on a transactional and experimental model, where knowers and known objects are not separated into metaphysical compartments, and any truths we come up with are workable and provisional solutions to problems. Dewey took this hypothesis to be generalizable across the disciplines; while the natural scientist in the laboratory may be taken as something of an exemplar, in principle, all intellectual investigation in the social sciences, the arts, and the humanities conforms to this general model. Philosophers do not grasp eternal verities or a priori certainties any more than literary theorists, psychologists, or historians do, and to assert this is not tantamount to skepticism but is an acknowledgment of the contingent and finite nature of our knowledge. Every form of it is an agonistic but ultimately cooperative search for the resolution to an experienced difficulty. We are social and rational beings all the way down, and our sociability and rationality are bound up together in a way that philosophy has often failed to see.

To speak of humanity as social means that we find ourselves embedded in a culture, a language, and a tradition of shared ideas and experiences, and that within the general domain of that within which we stand and participate situations arise that call for a mode of thought that is no "private soliloquy" but draws us into cooperative problem solving, the great exemplars of which are science and democracy. As he stated, "communication is not a bare emission of thoughts framed and completed in . . . solipsistic observation"; rather, "language and thought in their relation to signs and symbols are inconceivable save as ways of achieving concerted action."[36] Just as a new scientific idea is but a candidate for knowledge until it is communicated to and tested and confirmed by others, so a political proposal is but an opinion until it is discussed, applied, and found to work for the amelioration of a particular set of social conditions. Language is present from the beginning, and is "the agency by which other institutions and acquired habits are *transmitted*, and it *permeates* both the forms and the contents of all other cultural activities."[37] Rationality, pragmatically conceived, is an enterprise in language and experimentation whose fundamental orientation is toward resolving the myriad difficulties that arise in the course of experiences and practices that are socially shared.

The implications that Dewey's general conceptions of knowledge and experience would have for ethics, politics, education, aesthetics, and religion are the topics to which the following chapters turn.

Notes

1   Dewey, *Reconstruction in Philosophy*, MW 12 (1920), 144.

2   Dewey, *The Quest for Certainty*, LW 4 (1929), 232.

3   Dewey, *The Public and Its Problems*, LW 2 (1927), 345.

4   Dewey, *The Quest for Certainty*, LW 4 (1929), 142–3.

5   Dewey, "Review of F. C. S. Schiller's *Humanism: Philosophical Essays*," MW 3 (1904), 317.

6   Dewey, *Democracy and Education*, MW 9 (1916), 284.

7   Dewey, *The Quest for Certainty*, LW 4 (1929), 136, 29, 134.

8   Dewey, *Knowing and the Known*, LW 16 (1949), 52.

9   Dewey, *The Quest for Certainty*, LW 4 (1929), 235.

10 Dewey, *The Quest for Certainty*, LW 4 (1929), 157.

11 Dewey, "The Ethics of Animal Experimentation," LW 2 (1926), 101. Similar statements are found in MW 1, 129; MW 2, 58; MW 6, 78; and LW 5, 115.

12 Dewey, "Science as Subject-Matter and as Method," MW 6 (1910), 78.

13 Dewey, *The Quest for Certainty*, LW 4 (1929), 200.

14 Dewey, "Philosophy's Future in Our Scientific Age: Never Was Its Role More Crucial," LW 16 (1949), 379.

15 Dewey, "The School as Social Center," MW 2 (1902), 88.

16 Dewey, *Democracy and Education*, MW 9 (1916), 227; Dewey, *Individualism, Old and New*, LW 5 (1930), 88.

17 Dewey, "Is Logic a Dualistic Science?," EW 3 (1890), 75.

18 Dewey, *Reconstruction in Philosophy*, MW 12 (1920), 91, 239.

19 Dewey, "The Scholastic and the Speculator," EW 3 (1891), 153.

20 Dewey, *Knowing and the Known*, LW 16 (1949), 282.

21 Dewey, *How We Think*, LW 8 (1933), 318.

22 Dewey, "Foreword to *Argumentation and Public Discussion*," LW 11 (1936), 515.

23 Dewey, *The Quest for Certainty*, LW 4 (1929), 181.

24 Dewey, *Logic: The Theory of Inquiry*, LW 12 (1938), 108.

25 Dewey, *How We Think*, LW 8 (1933), 120, 121.120–1.

26 Dewey, *Experience and Education*, LW 13 (1938), 59.

27 Dewey, *How We Think*, LW 8 (1933), 227.

28 William James, *Pragmatism: A New Name for Some Old Ways of Thinking* (Harvard: Harvard University Press, 1981), 106, 42, 97, 97.

29 William James, *The Meaning of Truth* (Harvard: Harvard University Press, 1981), 47.

30 Dewey, *Reconstruction in Philosophy*, MW 12 (1920), 170.

31 Dewey, *Logic: The Theory of Inquiry*, LW 12 (1938), 15, 16.

32 While numerous texts have appeared on this general topic, an especially outstanding example is Louis Menand's *The Metaphysical Club: A Story of Ideas in America* (New York: Farrar, Straus, and Giroux, 2001).

33 Dewey, "Review of F. C. S. Schiller's *Humanism: Philosophical Essays*," MW 3 (1904), 317; Dewey, *Democracy and Education*, MW 9 (1916), 353–4.

34 Dewey, *Logic: The Theory of Inquiry*, LW 12 (1938), 4.

35 Dewey, *Reconstruction in Philosophy*, MW 12 (1920), 163.

36 Dewey, "The Inclusive Philosophic Idea," LW 3 (1928), 51.

37 Dewey, *Logic: The Theory of Inquiry*, LW 12 (1938), 51.

4

Ethics

Dewey's critics have long remarked upon a certain elusiveness in his work or indeed a vagueness that many have found frustrating. The vagueness charge is usually overstated and based on a less than careful reading of his texts, and in part it is likely based as well on the fact that so many of his ideas took shape over the course of several decades and found expression in a large number of works, ranging from lengthy treatises to short essays. His pragmatic experimentalism, for instance, was formulated and reformulated in several major works and a multitude of essays spanning half a century, and the same can be said of both his political and moral philosophies. No single work constitutes any kind of magnum opus on either subject, including the treatise that bears the rather imposing title of *Ethics* from 1932, although that book could be seen as a culmination of sorts of the ideas upon which he had been working throughout his career. The charge of vagueness greeted it as well. Anyone hoping to find in it an ethical system that could be compared to Kantian or utilitarian theory would be disappointed, and it would always be difficult to place his approach within the general field of modern philosophical ethics not only, as one scholar has noted, because "Dewey did not consolidate his ideas about ethics in any single work," but because "[t]he few books in which Dewey focused explicitly on ethics were textbooks and syllabi, written primarily for classroom work" and "were therefore not intended to be systematic theoretical formulations."[1]

Dewey's ethics is not vague, and the present chapter provides an analysis of this topic that will endeavor to clarify what he believed a philosophical ethics properly aims to provide and what it does not. Part of the confusion that has surrounded his approach to both moral and political theory is rooted in the difficulty of classifying his views with respect to the standard options of consequentialism and deontology, utilitarianism and Kantianism, intuitionism and virtue ethics, as well as liberalism and conservatism, socialism and Marxism, and so on. One might say none of the above if the question is into which theoretical camp Dewey readily fits and to which philosophers his position can be closely compared, although a closer reading finds him borrowing selectively from some of these. We begin with the premise that morality is not a kind of department that is separate from life or from the situations that we encounter in the course of our everyday dealings with human beings. Nor is the kind of inquiry that it enjoins removed from the empirical, the sociological, the literary, or the historical. An ethics that is not a castle in the air is not centered around "the purification of motives, edifying character, pursuing remote and elusive perfection, obeying supernatural command, acknowledging the authority of duty," or any similar idea that is centered around a state of personal being that is distinct from the conduct and situations that comprise one's life.[2] Ethics crucially bears not upon who one is in isolation but upon what one does in the context of social life and the mode of deliberation that we employ in resolving conflicts. It is particularistic in that its central question bears upon the good that can be accomplished in a given situation and the evils that can be avoided or remedied, and any general values or theoretical principles hold legitimacy only insofar as they are instrumental to ends that are essentially pragmatic. The moral pragmatist is not a blackboard philosopher but a problem-solver and an inquirer into what is to be done in resolving the conflicts that arise in the ordinary conduct of life. If frequently "[t]he ethical has been conceived in too goody-goody a way," with the consequence that it "does not reach down into the depths of the character-making agency," a better alternative is to thematize what in an early work he termed "social intelligence—the power of observing and comprehending social situations—and social power."[3]

Such an ethics does not proffer a set of hierarchically arranged values or a catalog of virtues, and his refusal to do so is one source of the charge of vagueness that Dewey's critics would level at him. His rationale for not providing one is that the good, whatever exactly this term is taken to mean, is not one. We shall return to the question of the good itself, but for now let us note that on his view the morally good is nothing transcending the meaning of the activity or situation in which we find ourselves. As he expressed it, "morals has to do with all activity into which alternative possibilities enter" since "wherever they enter a difference between better and worse arises. . . . The better is the good," or the good is the best or most meaningful course of action among the available alternatives in the case of a given conflict.[4] The best by what standard is a question about which Dewey was skeptical if we are speaking of a unified criterion such as the categorical imperative or the greatest happiness principle. Utilitarianism did lie in the neighborhood of what Dewey was proposing, and statements can be found in his writings in which he can appear to fall into this camp. The common good or general happiness is sometimes evoked at least implicitly in his ethical and political works, but the crucial point is that neither utility nor any comparable standard amounts to an absolute that can be abstracted from the concrete affairs of social life and to which we owe invariant allegiance. It may function as a principle in ethical inquiry, but as we shall see for Dewey all normative principles have the status of hypotheses rather than unconditional imperatives. Like the utilitarians, there is no doubting that in his moral and political writings he was speaking as one bent upon changing the world in sometimes radical ways, and with a general view toward some conception of the common good. His position could also be described as at least approximately consequentialist, but an important point of difference with the utilitarians is the latter's "assumption that there is a single, fixed and final good."[5] Given the complexity of human relations and conduct, the notion that in moral deliberation we must appeal in every circumstance to some unified standard, whether the general happiness or any other, is more likely to lead to the kind of rule fetishism of which Dewey was a lifelong opponent than to an optimal resolution to conflicts. A preoccupation with moral absolutes directs our attention in the wrong place, which is toward bringing the situation before us into conformity with a rule formulated in advance rather than resolving the difficulty. No theoretical model is able to keep up with the complex realities of moral conflict—from which it follows not that we ought to jettison ethical theory altogether but that our reflective efforts must award priority to situations themselves in their particularity and keep in view the often numerous values that are in play. A typical statement from Dewey along these lines is as follows:

> The office of deliberation is . . . to resolve entanglements in existing activity, restore continuity, recover harmony, utilize loose impulse and redirect habit. . . . Deliberation has its beginning in troubled activity and its conclusion in choice of a course of action which straightens it out. It no more resembles the casting-up of accounts of profit and loss, pleasures and pains, than an actor engaged in drama resembles a clerk recording debit and credit items in his ledger.[6]

Terms like "continuity," "harmony," and "straightens out" are purposely open-ended in meaning again because any attempt to spell them out in advance with the kind of analytical clarity that the utilitarian standard supplied leads to a misdirection of attention away from the situation itself and toward an abstraction. There is neither a single way to resolve ethical problems nor a guarantee that if we follow a given decision procedure we will get the right answer. No epistemology-centered conception of ethics is to be sought, if we intend by this a theoretical framework that prioritizes "how do you know" questions and a spirit of moral apriorism over an approach to conflicts that is more empirical and commonsensical. "Experience" in the field of moral philosophy "shows that the subordination of human good to an external and formal rule tends in the direction of harshness and cruelty."[7]

What, then, is the proper function of ethical theory if it is not to identify either an epistemological foundation for resolving conflicts, a particular set of values or conception of the good life, or a catalog of virtues or rules around which the moral life is to be organized? Part of the difficulty in answering this is that the mode of ethical theorizing that enlightenment thinkers assured us was both possible and necessary gave us an impossible standard by which to navigate the moral realm, leaving us to select among a now standard array of consequentialist, deontological, intuitionist, and other approaches each of which may hold a degree of insight but none of which captures the whole. For Dewey, it is not possible to state in advance of a given case of moral conflict in what its proper resolution consists for the reason again that there are simply too many variables to hold in view. Moral primacy always lies with the particular over the universal and the real over the ideal, yet he would not fly to the extreme of eliminating theoretical notions altogether. The mode of theorizing that he called for may be described as loosely empirical, particularistic, and situationalist, and where this last term does not mean relativistic. It does not follow from Dewey's claim that the good is not absolute that it is relative, whether it be to an individual situation or to anything at all, and nowhere did he suggest this. Instead he would make the case for a reflection that is, as he expressed it in an early work, "the study of *ethical relationships*, the study, that is, of this complex world of which we are members."[8] In a later work he would elaborate upon this as follows:

> Moral theory can (i) generalize the types of moral conflicts which arise, thus enabling a perplexed and doubtful individual to clarify his own particular problem by placing it in a larger context; it can (ii) state the leading ways in which such problems have been intellectually dealt with by those who have thought upon such matters; it can (iii) render personal reflection more systematic and enlightened, suggesting alternatives that might otherwise be overlooked, and stimulating greater consistency in judgment.[9]

Without eliminating the need for personal judgment, ethical theory can provide it with a preliminary orientation that is based upon similar conflicts that we have encountered before. Some generalization and contextualization that draw upon prior experience deliver us from a pure particularism, and "consistency in judgment" is no less important in the moral realm than in any other area of intellectual life where ideas need to cohere with other ideas, both our own and others'.

Incoherence or disagreement with respect to judgments of this order, and hence the need for ethical theory, increases, Dewey believed, in periods of rapid cultural change which include the era and society in which he was living. He would frequently remark that with increasing mobility, travel, urbanization, industry, and technology has come an unsettling of moral norms and customary practices, and a conflict of values that is "the most serious form of class warfare."[10] Dewey would never be nostalgic for time periods in which moral and cultural ideas were more readily agreed upon and would often speak in negative terms of such eras, but the loss of consensus around "solid and assured objects of belief and approved ends of action" creates special difficulties for modern societies in which ethical and political life becomes stratified along increasingly hostile lines.[11] "Each class is rigidly sure of the rightness of its own ends and hence not overscrupulous about the means of attaining them."[12] This sentence, which might have been written yesterday, takes us to the heart of Dewey's moral philosophy: while the forms of plurality that we are witnessing in the modern West is nothing to be lamented, societal and cultural change that is both rapid and vast does multiply the conflicts that necessitate a mode of inquiry for which standard ethical theories do not adequately prepare us. We regularly encounter situations in which conflicting goods pull us this way and that and we are compelled to weigh values, for instance, of personal and professional life. In cases of genuine doubt—brought on by a conflict more often of competing goods than of good and evil—seeing how others have navigated similar conflicts and the consequences that followed upon given courses of action rightly enters into our deliberations, and ethical theory accomplishes this on a larger scale and in a somewhat more abstract way than what we find in a more ordinary sort of reflection where we are weighing competing ends without looking up to a larger picture. Ethical theorizing paints such a picture without affording cut-and-dried solutions or removing the need for particularistic inquiry.

An ethics that is based upon experimental inquiry will represent a departure from a number of received ethical conceptions that include utilitarian and deontological approaches as well as traditional religious morality. The latter Dewey would often speak of in an educational context as a rather straightforward inculcation of divine precepts, where moral psychology comes down to an expectation of reward and a fear of punishment. About more sophisticated forms of religious ethics he would have relatively little to say, while a morality of custom would receive more explicit treatment, if primarily by way of contrast with the "reflective morals" that he was recommending. The centuries-long "transition from customary to reflective conduct" took us from an ethics that had been centered from prehistoric times around traditional values and norms to one rooted in either "conscience, reason, or . . . some principle which includes thought."[13] Noting that this distinction is relative rather than absolute, Dewey included ancient Greek moral philosophy in the latter category as well as Judeo-Christian thought since both approaches were displacing ancestral custom with an insight or a rationality that was individual as well as social. Reflective ethics in the modern period would accentuate the remediation of social ills over rule following, and it is this general trajectory that his own conception of ethical theory would try to extend. What he would deride as moralism may be understood as a relatively unreflective going along with whatever values or norms have been passed down between the generations, where personal conduct is essentially a matter of outward conformity to externally imposed requirements, while its antithesis gives us a more investigative model whose orientation is toward maximizing the good that can be obtained in given instances of moral conflict.

An ethics of reflection shifts the center of gravity away from values and rules that are fixed and often externally imposed toward a detailed and contextual inquiry into the many situations, behaviors, and conflicts that arise in modern life and which defy ready solution, where we are pulled in different directions by ends that are legitimate yet competing. What calls for reflection on such occasions encompasses everything from the motivations of persons to the history and meaning of our practices, the nature of our institutions, and the general attitudes and dispositions of those who are party to a given issue. The spirit of such reflection is resolutely undogmatic in that we are not applying a single yardstick inflexibly to every moral case we encounter but seeing particulars as particulars, which is in some ways analogous to others in our experience, in some ways unique, and in every case rich in complexity. We are drawing upon experiences both personal and socially shared while also going beyond them, regarding the case before us in light of such experience but in a preliminary way. Ethical reflection is empirical in that it foreswears all apriorism and observes closely the details of a given conflict and draws upon whatever insights it can from psychology, sociology, history, anthropology, and any other field that can enable us to get a hold on the case before us. Any judgment we form remains as subject to revision as a scientific hypothesis, as is commonly the case when we are practicing an art of juggling, arranging, and harmonizing various considerations, in this instance weighing competing values and giving each its due rather than reducing the manifold to a single end. As Dewey expressed it,

> The business of reflection in determining the true good cannot be done once for all, as, for instance, making out a table of values arranged in a hierarchical order of higher and lower. It needs to be done, and done over and over and over again, in terms of the conditions of concrete situations as they arise. In short, the need for reflection and insight is perpetually recurring.[14]

Ethical theory so conceived is procedural rather than substantive in the sense that its central concern lies with the method by which we resolve difficulties rather than a particular conception of the good life, while the method itself is a good deal more artful than more formalist decision procedures which, in principle, a machine could do. To speak of it as procedural does not entail that it is value-neutral, however, or that it jettisons received attitudes and principles, for indeed it does not. Moral customs and ideals, along with shared practices and habits, are fundamental to the moral life as Dewey understood it. For this deeply Hegelian thinker, social life in its totality "not only continues to exist *by* transmission, *by* communication, but it may fairly be said to exist *in* transmission, *in* communication. . . . What they must have in common in order to form a community or society are aims, beliefs, aspirations, knowledge—a common understanding," which includes substantive moral ends of one kind or another. One does not invent these out of nothing but largely inherits them in a tradition. As an example of this, Dewey mentions good manners as a kind of "minor morals" which one acquires by participating in customary forms of conduct rather than through rational inference: "Good manners come . . . from good breeding or rather are good breeding; and breeding is acquired by habitual action, in response to habitual stimuli," and in a social environment that is likewise habitual and formative.[15] The same is true of ethics in a more general sense. His point is not to downplay this but to emphasize that reflective morality regards all received ends as but a starting point of inquiry; the latter are myriad and in a good many situations conflicting, making it necessary to weigh one such end against another rather than regard traditional values as settling all ethical difficulties. Since customs themselves do not tell us what to do in the event of their conflict, we must regard them as the occasion for reflection and not its solution.

If we think of Dewey's ethics as a non-formalist proceduralism, one of its central distinctions is between rules and principles. For the former, he would have very little use, and he would frequently critique a good part of both traditional morality and moral education for an adherence to rules that he viewed as excessive and as shutting down inquiry where they ought to be informing it. If by a rule we mean an unconditional and inflexible standard of some kind, its "essential evil" as he saw it "is that it tends to render men satisfied with the existing state of affairs and to take the ideas and judgments they already possess as adequate and final."[16] Any system of rules makes it appear that the essential business of thinking has been accomplished by our predecessors, and all we need do is fall back upon the system rather than practice any real discernment of the case before us. When judging becomes a matter of heeding unconditional imperatives, the result is rigidity and ultimately authoritarianism, and his disdain for both would lead him to transform rules into principles which have the status of hypotheses rather than commands. The distinction turns not upon the content of a rule or principle—indeed we may regard any moral end in either light—but upon its spirit: are we treating the golden rule, for example, as an absolute requirement or as a possible solution to a particular conflict, and where the same may be asked of the virtues, of freedom or equality, and so on and so forth. A moral principle on Dewey's view does not dictate a particular course of action but is a tool by which to analyze a problematic situation; it is one relevant consideration among others and is more presumption than dogma.

Let us see how he formulates this distinction in the *Ethics*:

> *Rules are practical; they are habitual ways of doing things. But principles are intellectual; they are the final methods used in judging suggested courses of action.* The fundamental error of the intuitionalist is that he is on the outlook for rules which will of themselves tell agents just what course of action to pursue; *whereas the object of moral principles is to supply standpoints and methods which will enable the individual to make for himself an analysis of the elements of good and evil in the particular situation in which he finds himself.*

Remaining with our example of the golden rule: when modified into a principle, it supplies a "standpoint" or "method" of analysis in that without dictating a particular course of action it has us ask, what would happen in the case before us if we treated a particular person in the way we would want to be treated? What actions would this entail and what would the consequences be for the parties involved? Until we know the consequences, what we have is not moral knowledge but a hypothesis which might be true or false. Changing the example to equality, here is a value that can alternatively shed light by inquiring whether the parties to a given conflict have an equal opportunity to achieve their ends and what obstacles might skew this one way or another or it can treat equality as a rule whereby all parties must attain the same outcome regardless of any considerations apart from adherence to the rule. When equality becomes egalitarianism, or liberty libertarianism, or any value is regarded as an absolute that is imposed upon moral cases from without, trouble ensues. As he expressed it, "a violet and an oak tree are equal when one has the same opportunity to develop to the full as a violet which the other has as an oak," and not when they reach the same height.[17] The guidance such principles afford lies in the anticipation they create that certain kinds of situations are likely to be resolved satisfactorily by weighing one value more heavily than another on the grounds that when this has been tried in the past, the consequences have been found to be generally agreeable. That a given solution has worked well in the past is no guarantee that it will do so again, however, and does not remove the need to inquire anew into what it is likely to lead to, whether an exception ought to be made, or whether someone might have a better idea. As with any hypothesis, a principle evolves in constant interaction with new cases and is not frozen in time. It tells us not what to do but what to pay attention to and what questions to ask. Even the categorical imperative may be useful if it is regarded as a helpful device in analyzing moral situations rather than an axiom to which we owe complete obedience, and the same can be said of the principle of utility or any other.

The basic problem with rules formulated in advance of moral situations is that they take us away from experience and direct attention to abstract commands rather than the situations themselves. For Dewey, no ethical imperative is ever fully justified on a blackboard but must await confirmation in and by the individual cases to which it is applied. The latter hold a certain authority here, as in empirical inquiry it is the evidence gathered in a particular case that has primacy over a hypothesis formulated in advance. To speak of ethical principles as hypotheses or "methods of understanding" entails that their validity is in every case contingent on their applications and consequences.[18] They are not *a priori* certainties but "empirical generalizations from the ways in which previous judgments of conduct have practically worked out."[19] We can illustrate the point using the example of the principle of toleration. When regarded as a hypothesis grounded in prior experience we might approach a given conflict, let us say the question of same-sex marriage, as calling for an extension of traditional marital laws and norms to same-sex couples on the basis that relevantly similar conflicts—perhaps involving religion—have been resolved in the past in ways that all parties found they could live with even while many continued to harbor disapproval of particular attitudes or conduct. Our historical experience has been that tolerating some matters is much preferable to religious warfare and other forms of inter-group conflict which can sometimes deteriorate into violence. When viewed as a rule, toleration is an unconditional moral requirement where historical experience or any capacity to resolve conflicts to the general and partial satisfaction of all parties is beside the point. The point is the rule itself, which appears to the parties as an external imposition upon the conflict rather than a possibly useful method of coping with it. Moral knowledge in the latter case is something we can fall back upon without troubling ourselves with the consequences for human beings of our rule following, and it is this disregard for experience and situational contingency to which he would take exception.

As is always the case with Dewey, there is a spirit, if not of empiricism then of the empirical and the experiential, that reigns in his general approach to the ethical and the political and a resolute rejection of any form of apriorism. What matters in moral situations are values that are not outside of and imposed on situations themselves but are inherent to them. In any problematic situation that involves a conflict between persons, interests, or goods, what we are trying to determine is the "practical meaning of the situation," where this is initially indeterminate and must be investigated following the method of experimental inquiry. The practical meaning of a given conflict is nothing apart from "the action needed to satisfy it" to the general satisfaction of the parties involved. As he stated,

> There are conflicting desires and alternative apparent goods. What is needed is to find the right course of action, the right good. Hence, inquiry is exacted: observation of the detailed makeup of the situation; analysis into its diverse factors; clarification of what is obscure; discounting of the more insistent and vivid traits; tracing the consequences of the various modes of action that suggest themselves; regarding the decision reached as hypothetical and tentative until the anticipated or supposed consequences which led to its adoption have been squared with actual consequences. This inquiry is intelligence.[20]

Moral inquiry on this view is essentially a form of situational analysis in which what holds primacy is the situation itself over whatever abstract moral requirements may come to bear upon it. The difficulty is that the question of what is to be done in such situations is the opposite of self-evident as conflicting considerations, goods, and interests are in play and must be clarified and examined with a view to determining what course of action best resolves the difficulty without creating more problems than it solves. As for what abstract criteria determine when a moral problem has been satisfactorily resolved, there are no such criteria, and this is one of the main sources of the charge of vagueness. To a Kantian or a utilitarian, Dewey's refusal to provide such criteria appears as either a failure of nerve or simple confusion, but what we must keep in mind is his broad critique of the quest for certainty which so much modern, epistemology-centered philosophy engaged in with uninspiring results. Theorists like Kant and Mill created impossibly rationalistic standards on which to base ethical judgments, and standards that led by a straight line toward a rule fetishism that seemed to Dewey to hold greater regard for its axioms than the human beings upon whom they came to bear.

Many of his remarks upon this theme appear in texts that directly bear upon education in which the business of instilling a moral sensibility in the young is a perennial concern. How one imparts this sensibility is not through the direct application of rules but through a more or less empirical study of human relationships and conflicts where the teacher might pose a question, for instance, about how to relieve suffering in a given case. The question is not abstract—whether we ought to strive to relieve suffering in general, and if so, why—but particularistic: how might the suffering of this individual in these circumstances be relieved, given all the facts of the case and the options available to us? The next step in deliberation is to suggest a possible course of action, then to imagine how this is likely to play out and the consequences for any parties involved and to compare this against other alternatives. If the aim that is the occasion for our inquiry is to relieve someone's suffering, a satisfactory resolution will be the one that achieves this end more effectively than the alternatives without creating more difficulties down the line. "The end of the method," as he put it, " . . . is *the formation of a sympathetic imagination for human relations in action*; this is the ideal which is substituted for training in moral rules, or for analysis of one's sentiments and attitude in conduct."[21] What is being taught and learned are the complexities and vicissitudes of human relationships and the art of forming judgments in the everyday situations that we encounter, with an accent on particulars, meanings, and the ordinary goods that are at stake in such circumstances. The ethical here is regarded not as a realm separate from ordinary life but a method of coping with situations of a kind that we confront in the usual course of experience. One learns how to read situations and to do what they require and not to impose upon them moral imperatives that we have worked out in advance.

The trouble with general imperatives is that they are several in number and their meanings and implications are not immediately evident in the situations that we experience. The good is not one but many. Relieving suffering, pursuing happiness, the common good, altruism, freedom, creativity, friendship, toleration, and love are but several of the goods that human beings rightly pursue, and within any given case one or more such values may factor significantly and can pull us in conflicting directions. Many an ordinary conflict is not between good and evil but between one good and another, where it is not obvious which carries more weight in the circumstances and we must inquire into the probable consequences of actions A and B and from there judging which is to be preferred. The process is not formalistic but phronetic in a roughly Aristotelian sense, although Dewey would not draw heavily upon Aristotle's account of deliberation in the *Nicomachean Ethics*. That thinker, of course, would also maintain that the virtues are many and that moral reasoning is approximate, probabilistic, and oriented toward particulars, but despite Dewey's considerable knowledge of and frequent affinity for Platonic-Aristotelian thought, the extent to which he drew directly from this well is limited. The closest one finds to a general standard of the good in Dewey's ethical writings is the same concept of growth that would loom large in his philosophy of education. We shall return to this notion in Chapter 6, but for now let us define growth roughly as a process involving the cultivating of capacities of moral imagination and discernment, sympathy and compassion, and a judgment that can weigh conflicting goods in a way that is even-handed and reasonable if not finally demonstrable. Moral education is a development of qualitative perception, not computational capacity, and any growth in this area of mental life is in principle unending, as he would say of educational growth generally.

Ethical inquiry, we might say, is a continual search for the meaning and the good that is to be found in the midst of social conflict, or the least bad within it, while the good itself "consists in the meaning that is experienced to belong to an activity when conflict and entanglement of various incompatible impulses and habits terminate in a unified orderly release in action." Moral education by the same token "is learning the meaning of what we are about and employing that meaning in action." The good is continually spoken of as one with the meaning of a given situation, such that "[i]f we wished to transmute this generalization into a categorical imperative we should say: 'So act as to increase the meaning of present experience.'"[22] This, of course, is a simplification and not a rule for when we are speaking of the meaning of human action, we are speaking in qualitative terms and of meanings in the plural. Meaning is particular and situational; it is not the utility that is a standard knowable in a situational vacuum and which may be tallied using some purely quantitative measure.

Dewey would always refuse to create either an unconditional moral standard, a catalog of virtues, or a system of moral ends on a quasi-legal model, insisting always that identifying and doing the good in any real circumstance does not involve importing criteria from outside but finding what is optimal from within. No moral epistemology is to be had but for the kind of inquiry of which we have spoken. Fixed ends, fixed rules, or fixed anything is not to be found in a moral philosophy that owes more to common sense than to modern ethical theories which continue to oversimplify the moral domain by reducing it to either a method of problem-solving or a framework of universal values. Because no two cases are identical, "the good is never twice alike" and we are compelled to speak of the good not in its singularity but as indexed to particulars.[23] This may be readily seen in the case of meanings with which the good is so closely aligned. Two works of art, historical events, or human actions may exhibit meanings that are so intimately related that we are tempted to describe them as one, but they are not one. *Crime and Punishment* and *The Brothers Karamazov* are written by the same author, address closely related themes, and speak from a near-identical moral and aesthetic sensibility, but it remains that they are distinct works with distinct meanings. We must interpret the two differently, even as one offers more than a few clues as to how to read the other. Similarly, an act of friendship resembles another without being identical to it, and contingency abounds. Our offer to pay for a friend's lunch under one set of circumstances becomes a possible insult when circumstances change (our friend has become unemployed and is concerned about appearing a burden). Here one needs to think anew about whether to extend the offer, wishing to help out a friend without insulting him. The value of friendly generosity normally does not conflict with respecting their pride, but in this instance it may, causing us to inquire in Dewey's usual way how our friend will react if one offers to pay and if one does not. The proper course of action is not set in stone but is contingent upon this mode of questioning, and the search for the good is normally like this; it is an attempt to bring about a reconciliation of conflicting ends that is in some measure unique to the situation before us while also analogous to others we have encountered before and can learn from in a new set of circumstances. Moral deliberation is the opposite of myopic and focuses here upon intentions and there upon consequences, here upon short-term and there upon long-term consequences, here upon consequences for person X and there upon consequences for person Y, and is never the same twice. We are seeking a harmony that is not pre-established but optimal under a set of conditions that is in some measure unrepeatable.

One does not find in Dewey's ethical writings the usual dichotomies of egoism or altruism, rational calculation or intuitionism, or strict consequentialism or deontology, although on the latter issue he would tend to prioritize the consequences of human action over their intentions. Ethical deliberation as he conceived it is an art that strives to hold in view all such considerations and others besides, in short, any factor that is relevant to the question of what is to be done in a situation where ends that are usually compatible come into conflict for one reason or another and we are having to weigh competing considerations none of which can be dismissed beforehand. As a rule, deliberation tries to encompass more and more, which also includes both means and ends. That we deliberate about means is evident enough, but circumstances more than occasionally force us to deliberate about ends as well, most obviously when any two values appear to suggest incompatible actions and we are compelled to decide which value carries more weight, not in every case but in the one before us. We deliberate as well about both instrumental and intrinsic values. There are ends that, as Dewey put it, "are not good *for* anything; they are just goods," and the same can be said of evils.[24] Murder is an evil, full stop, just as love is good quite aside from how it might also be valuable as a means. All of this demands to be thought about whenever value X—whether instrumental or intrinsic, means or end—suggests a course of action that conflicts with value Y, and thought about both intellectually and emotionally. Regarding the latter, he would insist that "the consciousness of ends must be more than merely intellectual" but must include an "emotional responsiveness" which, while it is resistant to description, designates "the difference between the character which is hard and formal, and one which is sympathetic, flexible, and open. . . . We count upon [the latter] to accomplish more by tact, by instinctive recognition of the claims of others, by skill in adjusting, than the former can accomplish by mere attachment to rules."[25] Good judgment is not a purely calculative act but a situational responsiveness that occurs on an appropriate emotional register, and where again the contrast is with the absolutist for whom the moral life is a straightforward matter of heeding commands.

We have noted briefly the imaginative dimension of deliberation, and it is a theme that would carry a good deal of importance in Dewey's moral philosophy. The art of deliberation as he described it is multifaceted: it encompasses ends and means, instrumental and intrinsic values; it is embedded within customs and tradition; it is a social enterprise rather than a purely private capacity of mind; it is both cognitive and affective; and it is oriented toward problem-solving while also being an imaginative art. When Dewey spoke of moral imagination he was referring specifically to the activity of "dramatic rehearsal" which belongs to inquiry in general and connotes an anticipation of what is likely to follow in our experience upon a given action or hypothesis.[26] In the empirical case, if an hypothesis is true then we can anticipate that particular experiences should follow, and if our expectations are borne out then this counts toward its justification. In the moral case, imagination again takes the form of anticipating future experiences or playing out in one's mind what is likely to happen should one opt for action X rather than Y. I imagine my friend will not feel insulted by my offer to pay for lunch but will see my act as one of well-meaning generosity, which is then either confirmed or disconfirmed by my friend's response. In the activity of moral imagination, then, "We give way, *in our mind*, to some impulse; we try, *in our mind*, some plan. Following its career through various steps, we find ourselves in imagination in the presence of the consequences that would follow: and as we then like and approve, or dislike and disapprove, these consequences, we find the original impulse or plan good or bad." The advantage of this inward stage of the deliberative process "is that it is retrievable, whereas overt consequences . . . cannot be recalled."[27] Imaginative rehearsal allows us to anticipate experimentally and also quickly any number of actions before resolving on the one that is most likely to bring about an optimal resolution of whatever difficulty occasioned our inquiry.

Teaching and learning the art of deliberation so conceived is anything but straightforward, and Dewey would always warn against an approach to moral education that comes down to learning various dos and don'ts. The direct approach can be an efficient means of imparting information about societal norms, but it typically remains at a surface level of consciousness and fails to have the formative or transformative effect on the self that we tend to associate with an education of this sort. When we are not performing a purely intellectual exercise but learning to read moral situations and to discern what they require of us, history affords a more effective education than direct exhortation, depending of course on how history is taught. When the teacher's approach to the latter consists essentially in the piling up of information in the short-term memory as an end in itself, then its educational value is practically nonexistent and "the dead," as he was fond of repeating, "may be safely left to bury its dead." On the other hand, "when history is considered as an account of the forces in forms of social life," when "it shows the motives which draw men together and push them apart and depicts what is desirable and what is hurtful," history becomes an education in human relations.[28] It was Dewey's opinion that "social forces in themselves are always the same—that the same kind of influences were at work 100 and 1000 years ago that are now," from which it follows that if we wish to learn about human relations in their full complexity, it is best to study the past, when the basic forces and dynamics that governed social life were the same as at present and we have the benefit of hindsight as to what resolutions to whatever conflicts arose worked out over the larger course of time and which did not.[29] History also presents us with a simpler interpretation of events than is ever possible in the present, which again promotes the educational end of getting a hold on social conflicts by directing attention in the right way, toward the motivations, dynamics, and forces that drive human beings to do the things that they do, and in light of this toward solutions to the conflicts such forces continually generate. When the past is seen not as something that is over and done with but a reflection of the present, it is a form of sociology whose relevance and vitality lie in the perspective it offers on our own times. A focused narrative account of some past conflict provides a level of informational detail that is sufficient for the educational purpose without overwhelming us with the bewildering array of facts with which present experience often confronts us, facts that must be selectively ordered and interpreted before we are able to reflect upon them in the critical way that moral education prizes. Literature can be equally conducive to this end, as he would point out. Here as well one finds a level of complexity and narrative development over time that illuminates human relations in a richer way than is often possible through the study of real-world conflicts. Not only the problem-solving art but the art of discernment, deliberation, and appreciation which has a formative influence on the young is often more teachable and learnable, Dewey believed, through an exposure to literature than by the more direct means that moral educators have traditionally employed.

A couple of final themes that bear mention are Dewey's conceptions of individualism and the self. Both topics feature quite prominently in his ethical writings, and if there is an important sense in which this Hegelian thinker was not an individualist there is a quite different sense in which he was. His *Individualism, Old and New* of 1930 would find Dewey criticizing severely an older form of American individualism that was centered around wealth and class while making the case for a new individualism in which the potentialities of the person are given their moral due while conceptualizing these as fully integrated with a social system in which the individual is a thoroughgoing participant. That text would find him lamenting the "submergence of the individual" in modern life in the sense that in the name of an individualism that promised liberation from tradition, ignorance, and poverty in the form of an industrial capitalism in which every man and woman could achieve their full potential, by the twentieth century this had hardened into a corporate mentality that prized wealth and social climbing excessively and with them new forms of conformity which hoisted individualism on its own petard. One found oneself increasingly submerged in forms of social life in which opportunities for self-fashioning and self-expression were few, the individual retreated into pleasures and pursuits that were alienating and vapid, and one fell into an "artificially induced uniformity of thought and sentiment [which] is a symptom of an inner void."[30] Experiences of social life were ever less of meaningful participation and connection and were replaced with an empty sameness of belief and behavior which effectively transformed individualism into its opposite.

Never one to fly between extremes, Dewey's prescription was not to reject individualism but to reconceptualize it in an overtly democratic spirit. "To gain an integrated individuality," as he put it,

> each of us needs to cultivate his own garden. But there is no fence about this garden: it is no sharply marked-off enclosure. Our garden is the world, in the angle at which it touches our own manner of being. By accepting the corporate and industrial world in which we live, and by thus fulfilling the pre-condition for interaction with it, we, who are also parts of the moving present, create ourselves as we create an unknown future.[31]

Individuality in Dewey's new individualism is fundamentally a participation in the democratic life of one's society, not in a narrow political connotation but in the sense of an active engagement in the broader ethos of one's culture. One creates a harmony between one's own talents and interests and the larger social good in a manner that constitutes no sacrifice of the person to the collective or vice versa. Individualism in this sense is not the opposite of altruism and indeed is virtually indistinguishable from it; it seeks one's own conception of the good in constant interaction with the ways and practices of a culture that is unified but not so tightly unified as to preclude innovation. The common good may be the standard by which the individual's contribution is assessed, but this standard itself "demands the full development of individuals in their distinctive individuality, not a sacrifice of them to some alleged vague larger good under the plea that it is 'social.'"[32] Here again Dewey would defend the dialectic over any opposition between self-realization and the social good, while any individualism must be encompassed within a larger democratic philosophy to which we shall return in the next chapter.

Regarding the self, Dewey conceived this as a being that is always in the making and that is one with habitual action. There is no determinate entity, be it a material or ideal being, that is the human person in its capacity as a moral agent, but a self that comes to be what it is in the mode of action and over the course of time. The central notion here is character. The word itself is a noun, but to what does it refer but our actions, specifically those that we engage in repeatedly through time and that settle into habits which afford the self a consistency and an element of predictability. Characters come in many forms, of course, and a vital distinction is between those that run in a thousand contradictory directions and those that exhibit an integration of actions, motivations, habits, and social roles into something that is stable and coherent. In ethical deliberation, what is in question is at once what is the most good that can be achieved in the situation before us and, inseparable from this, "what kind of person one is to become, what sort of self is in the making, what kind of a world [one] is making."[33] A good character is one with its conduct, and where the latter term connotes not actions in general but those that demonstrate some constancy of meaning and motivation. The latter is what the self is known by and known as; one is the person who has pursued this or that end and the one who can be counted upon to continue this into the future. One is, morally speaking, what one does habitually through life, not in a mechanical way but organically; the various ends that one pursues and the ways one pursues them hang together in some way, as the organs of a body work together to achieve a common purpose while remaining distinct. When one acts in a moral context, one is going to work on the situation and on oneself in the same gesture, shaping and sometimes reshaping the self one has been, and ideally striving to bring about an integration of the self that is a moral achievement and a very difficult one. Constancy of motivation and conduct, for Dewey, is not an accomplishment if directed toward the wrong ends, but when it is bound up with the pursuit of the good the result is a character that is both stable and exemplary.

While, as we have noted, Dewey would always place a certain importance on consequences, there is no true separation between these and the intentions of the agent for on his account of the moral life it is all of the above—motivations, short- and long-term consequences, habitual activity, practices, principles, tradition— that are in play in the art of deliberation. As common sense plainly knows, intentions matter, but they are not uniquely and supremely authoritative, and the same is true of consequences. Everything matters, both what we do in the world, whether intentionally or unintentionally, and the kind of character we fashion in the process. "The conclusion," he would state,

> is that conduct and character are strictly correlative. Continuity, consistency, throughout a series of acts is the expression of the enduring unity of attitudes and habits. Deeds hang together because they proceed from a single and stable self. . . . [T]he essence of reflective morals is that it is conscious of the existence of a persistent self and of the part it plays in what is externally done.

It is as true to say of our actions that they form the self as that they reveal it, that they exhibit the character of the person while never losing a potentiality to transcend this and to overcome the self one has been. The self that one is is always also in the making, and every moral situation is an occasion for a kind of redemption, to live down the past or to continue building a character that is unified and worthy of admiration. The Aristotelian note here was not lost on Dewey. A virtuous person is one with their actions, and

> [t]he attainment of consequences reacts to form the self. Moreover, as Aristotle said, the goodness of a good man shines through his deeds. . . [T]he self is more than a cause of an act in the sense in which a match is a cause of a fire; . . . the self has entered so

intimately into the act performed as to qualify it. The self reveals its nature in what it chooses.[34]

Dewey's ethics is one part of a larger social philosophy which includes a theory of education and a political philosophy, and it is to these topics that we turn in the next pair of chapters.

Notes

1 Gregory F. Pappas, "Dewey's Ethics: Morality as Experience" in *Dewey: Interpretations for a Postmodern Generation*, ed. Larry Hickman (Bloomington: Indiana University Press, 1998), 100.

2 Dewey, *Human Nature and Conduct*, MW 14 (1922), 194.

3 Dewey, "Ethical Principles Underlying Education," EW 5 (1897), 75.

4 Dewey, *Human Nature and Conduct*, MW 14 (1922), 193.

5 Dewey, *Reconstruction in Philosophy*, MW 12 (1920), 172.

6 Dewey, *Human Nature and Conduct*, MW 14 (1922), 139.

7 Dewey, *Ethics*, LW 7 (1932), 249.

8 Dewey, "Teaching Ethics in the High School," EW 4 (1893), 60.

9 Dewey, *Ethics*, LW 7 (1932), 166.

10 Dewey, *Human Nature and Conduct*, MW 14 (1922), 58.

11 Dewey, *Individualism, Old and New*, LW 5 (1930), 66.

12 Dewey, *Human Nature and Conduct*, MW 14 (1922), 59.

13 Dewey, *Ethics*, LW 7 (1932), 162–3.

14 Dewey, *Ethics*, LW 7 (1932), 212.

15 Dewey, *Democracy and Education*, MW 9 (1916), 7, 22.

16 Dewey, *Ethics*, LW 7 (1932), 282.

17 Dewey, *Ethics*, LW 7 (1932), 280, 346.

18 Dewey, *Reconstruction in Philosophy*, MW 12 (1920), 172.

19 Dewey, *Human Nature and Conduct*, MW 14 (1922), 165.

20 Dewey, *Reconstruction in Philosophy*, MW 12 (1920), 173.

21 Dewey, "Teaching Ethics in the High School," EW 4 (1893), 57.

22 Dewey, *Human Nature and Conduct*, MW 14 (1922), 148, 194, 196.

23 Dewey, *Human Nature and Conduct*, MW 14 (1922), 148.

24 Dewey, *Democracy and Education*, MW 9 (1916), 250.

25 Dewey, "Moral Principles in Education," MW 4 (1908), 288–9.

26 Dewey, *Human Nature and Conduct*, MW 14 (1922), 132.

27 Dewey, *Ethics*, LW 7 (1932), 275.

28 Dewey, "History for the Educator," MW 4 (1909), 192.

29 Dewey, "Ethical Principles Underlying Education," EW 5 (1897), 71.

30 Dewey, *Individualism, Old and New*, LW 5 (1930), 66, 83.

31 Dewey, *Individualism, Old and New*, LW 5 (1930), 122–3.

32 Dewey, *Ethics*, LW 7 (1932), 348.

33 Dewey, *Human Nature and Conduct*, MW 14 (1922), 150.

34 Dewey, *Ethics*, LW 7 (1932), 172, 287.

5

Liberal Politics

Dewey's critics have long complained of vagueness in his political writings, and perhaps an appropriate avenue into his thought in this area is to consider the basis of a charge that was issued from both the left and the right. Ideologues at both ends of the spectrum are often impatient with talk of situationalism, contextualism, or consequentialism as it can appear to the committed as faint-heartedness. When one steps back from Dewey's enormous output of writing on a wide range of political themes over several decades and looks for a larger picture, such a picture does come into view, but not in the way of a Marx or a Mill. If we are intent upon getting an easy handle on his political philosophy, frustration does ensue, and terms such as the ones mentioned have often been resorted to for a few reasons. The first is that socialists and conservatives will both find Dewey expressing numerous criticisms of their positions on a number of issues. A second is his own reluctance to assign a label to his political stance but for the rather enigmatic "democracy" or "liberal democracy." A classical liberal in the mode of Locke, the American founders, Mill, and so on, he was in some respects and was not in others, while a liberal progressivist in the manner of Green, Hobhouse, and Hobson, he also was in some respects and was not in others. Not a very helpful description, it might be said. A third reason is Dewey's refusal to articulate an unambiguous set of political principles or doctrines in a similar manner as his refusal to propose a catalog of ethical virtues. A fourth reason is that the two refusals were similarly motivated: what matters in the case of political judgments is not their conformity with rules or values spelled out in advance but their capacity to resolve social problems of one kind or another and the quality of deliberation that generates them, and we are back to the contextualism or situationalism with which the more ideological will always be unsatisfied. It is also not quite accurate to assign these labels, for Dewey did defend a set of political principles and values which, in a preliminary way at least, do admit of abstract formulation, and we are not approaching either ethical or political questions in a purely ad hoc manner. What is central throughout his rather voluminous political writings, from the major works to the countless shorter essays, is again the theme of inquiry where policies are determined in every case by their capacity to remedy social ills.

Dewey has long been designated a political liberal, and we may retain the description provided we resist the impulse to place him in a pigeonhole alongside others who bear that label. If he was a liberal, he was an unusual one, and likely in a way that does him credit. His focus was always on concrete issues and methodology far more than on developing a settled position somewhere on the spectrum of left and right—although it is not difficult to glean a tendency in his political thought toward the moderate left. A Marxist he decidedly was not, and while it is not unusual to find him appealing to classical liberal values, he was no conservative. We shall return to the question of Dewey's liberalism, but for now let us begin by remarking that democracy (American but also Western democracy more generally) was always at the center of Dewey's concerns when questions of social philosophy (political, ethical, educational, and even epistemological) arose, and in both his more systematic treatments of political philosophy as well as his shorter pieces which were directed variously toward an academic and a more public readership. When he called for "the use of intelligence to judge consequences," the consequences upon which political judgments rightly depend are those bearing upon specific conflicts and difficulties as well as the larger condition of a democratic order.[1] If "analytic observation of actual interactions to determine the elements operative on each side and their consequences is not easy . . . to execute," it remains a basic imperative of political reasoning that is properly oriented toward the concrete more than the abstract.[2]

As with so much of his philosophy, at the heart of Dewey's liberalism is a distinctive conception of democracy which has often been imperfectly termed "participatory." It indeed demands a broad involvement of citizens in the deliberation and formation of public policy, but more important than the percentage of the citizenry that participates in the democratic process is the nature of the process itself and the quality of deliberation that it practices. He sets out from the more or less Hegelian premise that "men are held together by the relations that proceed from and that manifest an ultimate cosmic mind," and proposes that "the basis of society and the state is shared intelligence and purpose, not force nor yet self-interest."[3] These two partial sentences from *Liberalism and Social Action* say much, beginning with an ontology of social life and proceeding into a political theory that is consistent with it. His variation of post-Kantian idealism is an important premise in his conception of democracy for the society he envisions is not one of Hobbesian atoms but of organically and rationally interacting citizens for whom democracy is less a set of institutions than an ethos and "a way of life."[4] Without affinities of culture, values, and community, a democratic order does not take root but can only be grafted on in a manner that is unlikely to succeed. "The clear consciousness of a communal life," in his words, "in all its implications, constitutes the idea of democracy," while without this consciousness, principles of freedom, equality, or anything else will be "hopeless abstractions."[5] Elsewhere he would remark that "[r]egarded as an idea, democracy is not an alternative to other principles of associated life. It is the idea of community life itself."[6] This is not a strong communitarianism but a conception of associated living, the core of which is a pragmatic and public-spirited inquiry into the remediation of social ills.

Dewey's political philosophy may be understood as an elaboration of the details and implications of this preliminary definition of democracy, beginning with this ethos itself. Citizens of a democracy are not true egoists but individuals whose capacities and life plans are organically sustained by a social order in which they stand as participants. Hobbesian and utilitarian moral psychology is rejected in favor of a civic-mindedness that draws no sharp division between self-interest and public-spiritedness. Neither a strong altruism nor egoism is presupposed, and indeed Dewey did not regard human nature and motivation in terms of this opposition. We shall return to the notion of the "great community" later, but a human community with a potential for democratic institutions practices a way of life that elicits individual powers of thought and behavior without authoritarianism. Drawing upon a store of shared knowledge and experience, it affords as many opportunities as possible for citizens to participate in collective decision-making, a good deal of which consists either in adapting received knowledge to novel situations or in reconsidering old ways in light of circumstances they did not foresee. "In theory," as Dewey expressed it, "the democratic method is persuasion through public discussion carried on not only in legislative halls but in the press, private conversations and public assemblies. The substitution of ballots for bullets, of the right to vote for the lash, is an expression of the will to substitute the method of discussion for the method of coercion." It seeks "to keep factional disputes within bounds" while recognizing that plurality of thought is an ineliminable feature of any human community.[7] In a democratic society, legitimate disagreement of opinions and values may be compared to a river flowing between banks that are relatively stable and which consist in the agreements our predecessors arrived at and which go by the name of tradition. If a political conservative or traditionalist Dewey was not, it remains that current deliberations must draw upon the inquiries of prior generations—even while the latter are not sacrosanct—and work toward the amelioration of current social ills in this light. The earlier distinction between discussion and coercion, or ballots and bullets, gets us to the heart of the matter: a democratic way of life multiplies opportunities for collective inquiry and problem-solving beyond what is customary and neither conforms blindly to the past nor abolishes it in the name of a revolutionary ideology. What he called "the mediating function of liberalism is all one with the work of intelligence. This fact is the root . . . of the emphasis placed by liberalism upon the role of freed intelligence as the method of directing social action."[8]

A well-functioning democracy requires a quality and degree of public participation both of which, in Dewey's estimation, were lacking in the American democracy of his time. Low voter turnout rate is one obvious indicator of the apathy that is fatal to the kind of participatory order he was calling for, as is a less than vigorous resistance to the backsliding into authoritarianism to which any social order is susceptible and also the vulnerability to propaganda which he believed to be widespread. This last point is especially problematic if we wish to conceive of inquiry as a fully rational and cooperative social practice, for propaganda, like sophistry, poisons the well upon which a democratic citizenry depends for information about what is happening in the society and manipulates information and viewpoints to accord with the interests of those controlling the instruments of propaganda. News organizations in particular distort events to instill whatever opinions they prefer and by means both covert and subtle: "Favorable and unfavorable presentation of individuals, laudation and ridicule, subtle suggestion of points of view, deliberate falsification of facts and deliberate invention of half-truth or whole falsities, inculcate by methods, of which those subject to them are not even aware, the particular tenets which are needed to support private and covert policies."[9] States, of course, may and often do likewise, as may any who possess the instruments of public persuasion. This is a serious matter for Dewey in view of the importance that public opinion carries in the political order he envisioned and its susceptibility to manipulation. Gullibility in the face of propaganda would become a key issue that his theory of education would attempt to remedy, as we shall see, but it is also a sizeable political problem for any democratic order in which the means of propaganda are held by particular actors. Naivety and docility of mind undermine a social order that values both robust participation rights and participation of a relatively demanding kind.

How Dewey's liberalism relates to its more classical forms is not a straightforward proposition. From its inception in the seventeenth and eighteenth centuries, liberalism enjoined certain forms of social participation, but Dewey's contentions were that as historical conditions change, the requirements of democratic citizenship change with them, while principles adapted to one set of socioeconomic conditions require modification when the circumstances change. Classical liberal values of individuality and freedom, including the free expression of ideas, continue to endure in twentieth-century life, but the accent upon property rights and free market economics reflects the realities of another time and does not account for the rise of vested economic interests which threaten to overwhelm a democratic order. Under frontier conditions, notions of rugged individualism, self-reliance, property, and contract carried an importance that was in some ways time-bound and applying them unrevised to modern conditions is less a liberal than a conservative posture. Political principles are not sacrosanct but are more or less useful solutions to the problems that exist at a given time and place, and while some of them will endure across generations and centuries, others will generate new difficulties and require either reinterpretation or replacement. Personal freedom and indeed rugged individualism carry an importance that transcends the realities of eighteenth-century America, but what varies is the meaning and implications of such values:

> At one time, liberty signified liberation from chattel slavery; at another time, release of a class from serfdom. During the late seventeenth and early eighteenth centuries in meant liberation from despotic dynastic rule. A century later in meant release of industrialists from inherited legal customs that hampered the rise of new forces of production. Today, it signifies liberation from material insecurity and from the coercions and repressions that prevent multitudes from participation in the vast cultural resources that are at hand.[10]

A laissez-faire liberal Dewey was not on grounds that the socioeconomic realities of twentieth-century America were that the liberty of a sizeable share of the population was being undermined by new forms of economic oppression brought on by capitalism. Classical liberalism had shaded into an economic conservatism which saw no significant role for the state in remedying economic inequalities and attendant social ills which had assumed increasing importance in American life. The "new liberalism" of his time was addressing this by advocating the kind of measures that would lead to the welfare state and the sizeable leftward turn which, in the case of Dewey and many others, would involve flirting with socialism.

Classical liberals, he believed, had become absolutists about a set of policies that effectively remedied the absolutism of that era but which were no longer responsive to numerous difficulties of modern life.

Promoting freedom no longer meant leaving the individual alone but fostering conditions that would enable "effective liberty of thought and action" in contrast with the "purely formal or legal liberty" prized by liberalism in its original form.[11] Effective freedom he would define, as so many twentieth-century liberals would not in primarily "negative" terms as a general right against harm at the hands of individuals or the state but more broadly or "positively" as a right to live under conditions variously political, legal, and economic that are optimally suited to the pursuit of happiness. These conditions are as contingent as human nature itself—which again would represent a significant departure from an earlier liberal philosophy for which the human being bears a universal and unchanging nature. Metaphysical conceptions of the latter, as we find them in Hobbes, Locke, Bentham, and so on, Dewey would abandon for a more Hegelian view, emphasizing the embeddedness of the individual within a historical community, which is also the ground from which ethical and political values emerge. Metaphysical materialism, psychological egoism, and the social contract he would jettison along with popular conceptions of the will to power (vaguely attributable to Nietzsche) as the animating principle of human behavior. Hobbes' war of all against all is not the natural condition of human beings, nor would Dewey be quick to replace this with any simple alternative. His understanding of human nature is an amalgam of ideas borrowed from Hegel, Green, and Darwin, among major figures, and it is social all the way down. He wanted no part of either social Darwinism or Marxism, and instead took the view that "while there are native organic or biological structures that remain fairly constant, the actual 'laws' of human nature are laws of individuals in association, not of beings in a mythical condition apart from association."[12] Apart from biological constants, there is no separating human nature from culture, and no separating the latter from the values that "arise from the relations which human beings intimately sustain to one another, . . . [while] their authoritative force springs from the very nature of the relation that binds people together."[13] No political values are grounded in either human nature or natural law if either is conceived as something universal or frozen in time, although he would reject cultural relativism as well. Most classical liberal values—the most obvious exception being free market economics—survive in Dewey's liberalism, as does democracy itself, but variably according to the societal circumstances in which such values are upheld. Had capitalism succeeded in lifting all boats rather than creating what he regarded as unacceptable disparities of wealth, he would presumably have defended it as well, but such matters are judged by the consequences for all upon whom they come to bear and not by means of a hypothetical social contract or a metaphysics of human nature. Human nature is not an unchangeable given but is culturally variable. As he would express this important point, "while certain needs in human nature are constant, the consequences they produce (because of the existing state of culture—of science, morals, religion, art, industry, legal rules) react back into the original components of human nature to shape them into new forms. The total pattern is thereby modified."[14] The key notion here again is interaction: nature and culture interact dynamically and are not external to each other, while the particulars of human relations are entailments of this basic structure.

Whether Dewey was in any sense an individualist may be answered in the affirmative, but again with a difference. Individualism in its Hobbesian form does not withstand scrutiny on a number of grounds while its American eighteenth- and nineteenth-century formulations reflect a pioneer and commercial spirit that no longer suits the conditions of modern life. By Dewey's time, individualism carried a primarily economic connotation which was, in his view, a vestige of an earlier period which ill-suited an increasingly urban, industrial, and secular civilization. What he called the "tragedy of the 'lost individual'" is that the deep social ties that in former times afforded an orientation toward life have been replaced by existentially vacuous associations which do not penetrate into the affective and imaginative dimension of our lives. If the old synthesis of Christian values, natural rights, and capitalism now rings hollow, it must be replaced by a new individualism that places an accent upon democratic forms of sociability in which any dichotomy of individualism and collectivism is lost. Individualism in its traditional form maintained that one is optimally free in being left alone while the new "creative individuality" that he preferred speaks of an "[o]riginality and uniqueness [which] are not opposed to social nurture" but instead "are saved by it from eccentricity and escape."[15] This is an individualism of mind which prizes creative participation in practices that are invariably social and in its political forms involves cooperation between state, business, and labor on a model that again flirts with socialism without unambiguously embracing it. Any individualism that is worth conserving would be one that is not restricted to the members of an affluent class but may be partaken of by the citizenry in general, and this can only be an individualism of thought and association. Never one to reject one extreme for the other, his rejection of the individualism of old did not entail any form of collectivist politics but rather led to the view that

> every individual is to share in the duties and rights belonging to control of social affairs, and, . . . social arrangements are to eliminate those external arrangements of status, birth, wealth,

sex, etc., which restrict the opportunity of each individual for full development of himself. On the individual side, it takes as the criterion of social organization and of law and government release of the potentialities of individuals. On the social side, it demands cooperation in place of coercion, voluntary sharing in a process of mutual give and take, instead of authority imposed from above.[16]

It remains on his account both that "society consists in the last analysis only of individual persons" and that the latter retain moral authority over the collective, even as no grand opposition emerges from this.[17]

Whether one classifies Dewey as a liberal individualist or socialist is undoubtedly less important than the content of his political philosophy, and different texts find him claiming now one label and now another. Insofar as the designation of liberal applies to him, he was not, as we have suggested, a classical liberal in the mold of Locke, Kant, Mill, or Hayek, but was part of a movement of new liberals or progressives that included Green and Hobhouse and which leaned toward the moderate (not the hard) left. Authoritarian socialism, particularly in its Marxian form, held no appeal for Dewey, and a revolutionist he was not. Democracy in his sense of the word lies at the center of liberal politics, and it remains liberal insofar as individual freedom is among our fundamental values and a primary function of the state is to "make possible effective liberty and opportunity for personal growth in mind and spirit in all individuals."[18] The realization of individual talents and the pursuit of happiness are about as sacrosanct as any among the political values of a liberal democracy, and they align with values of free inquiry and diversity of viewpoint that are necessary preconditions of a democratic way of life, and where the latter connotes a form of social organization and an ethos in which all have a right and an obligation to proffer ideas and to debate with their fellow citizens the issues of the day, whether it be in large public fora or in everyday conversation with friends or neighbors. Informal ("intelligent") communication is the lifeblood of a democracy, and a good part of public policy is properly oriented toward bringing about the conditions that render it possible for all.

At his most radical (which was not especially radical or, at any rate, extreme), Dewey would assert that a "renascent liberalism" must reorient its educational institutions in ways that train the young for democratic participation—a topic to which we shall return in the chapter to follow—and affect a degree of institutional change that goes beyond the piecemeal. Some of the institutional and public policy changes this would entail Dewey did address, albeit most often in a particularistic way in texts such as *The Public and Its Problems* and *Liberalism and Social Action* and in countless short pieces addressed variously to academic and public audiences. The larger picture of what kind of democratic order he envisioned is slightly difficult to get into focus, contingent as it is upon the ongoing course of public deliberation and the particular accommodations that a citizenry may reach at a given time, while the banks of the river would remain relative constants. The banks or principles themselves are drawn from the larger historical tradition and reflect values of equal freedom and participation rights but nothing resembling an ideology. A state ought not uphold the kind of creed that a political party would but may be thought of as a forum in which the clash of viewpoints serves the general purpose of remedying the ills of the society while promoting "actual as distinct from merely legal liberty."[19]

There is no doubting that Dewey was a staunch defender of many of the liberties traditionally associated with liberal philosophy. Free market economics is the obvious exception, but freedom of speech, expression, conscience, religion, assembly, association, and a free press would remain as inviolable in his iteration of American liberalism as in any earlier formulations. Each of these liberties falls under the umbrella of free inquiry, and even a market economy he would not reject completely but instead harness to the public will in a manner that did not amount to a command economy. A mixed economy he preferred to the laissez-faire model, as so many liberals of his era and beyond would also do, but principles of free speech, expression, and so on are indispensable ingredients of a democratic order for reasons that are not far to seek. Rational inquiry requires free minds that can propose and test any and all hypotheses, all of which must be held to the same epistemic standards and subjected to rigorous questioning and debate. Political proposals are no different in this way than hypotheses put forward in any other field and must run the same gauntlet of criticism that knowledge in every region of experience does. Ballots over bullets is the method, but ballots themselves are not (or should not be) mere preferences but conclusions reached in a debate in which all are called upon to participate. The indication of what in an educational context he would call "a liberal mind" is not that one merely holds particular opinions but is instead "the *way* in which they are reached and accepted."[20] They are not absolutes but pragmatic and contingent resolutions to conflicts that a social order has encountered in the past. A right of free speech "works" pragmatically in the sense that it is a necessary condition of a social order whose central business is the amelioration of social difficulties and conflicts. It is on his account not less but more secure a right than it was in classical liberalism where it was viewed as a negative right to speak as one will without fear of censure. As an individual good, such a right is forever subject to the vagaries of a potentially hostile majority, while on Dewey's account free speech is a social good which as such is less likely to be seen as at odds with the common good and is thus more secure than hitherto. When freedom of expression becomes a right "to share in joint conference and consultation on social questions and issues" rather than a purely individual good whose inveterate tendency is to upset the majority, it is more deeply integrated into a democratic order rather than an external threat to it.[21]

A democracy conceived as a community of inquiry requires an advanced degree of toleration of ideas, attitudes, and expressions with which any of its members, whether a minority or a majority, disagree, and toleration is more forthcoming when what we reject or disapprove of is regarded as part of the fabric of a democracy in which we all participate. It requires as well expansive freedom of thought "because the essence of the democratic principle is appeal to voluntary disposition instead of to force, to persuasion instead of coercion." Toleration and freedom of thought are both undermined by the attitude that we already know in what the good or the truth consists and can accordingly proscribe contrary opinions, and it is an attitude that is not limited to dictatorships or aggressive majorities. In democratic societies, he remarked, "[t]he real culprit is always some powerful minority which prefers to use methods of suppressive force or of perversion and degradation of opinion by means of propaganda."[22] The tendency toward factionalism and oligarchy is the proverbial wolf at the door of any democratic order, and the remedy to it remains the classical liberal one of securing broad rights of free expression, only now regarded as a "social asset" rather than "something inhering in individuals apart from and even in opposition to social claims."[23]

Where his liberal credentials may come into question is on the issue of social planning. As a political thinker, it is fair to say that Dewey had more the mind of an engineer than a utopian. No classless society or shining city on a hill is to be found in his writings, and on the whole his approach to political questions tends toward the piecemeal and quotidian. He placed a degree of confidence in what we would now call social engineering than liberals hitherto would have approved, although it is important to avoid conflating a couple of senses of the idea of social planning. The planned society on the model of Soviet Russia and other authoritarian states centralizes all social engineering activities in accordance with a scheme that is enforced by law in top-down fashion. If it is modern, it is sure to speak in the name of science and scientific expertise, although this claim is likely to be spurious. Dewey's planning society, by contrast, is neither centralized, top-down, expertocratic, nor authoritarian. He was not recommending that a cadre of elites, be they politicians, scientists, technocrats, or ostensible experts of one kind or another, be empowered to engineer any or all aspects of the society, although some of his critics mistakenly took him to be endorsing this. Nor is any blueprint worked out at some remove from the democratic process capable of resolving the ills of society provided it be implemented without impediment or that it gains a degree of buy-in from the voters. The planning society he was speaking of is one in which the people alone hold the reigns of the democracy while inquiring on a cooperative basis into the remediation of whatever problems the public faces. Effective planning requires ongoing adjustments in the formation of public policy and input not only from experts but from any citizens and groups who care to participate in public decision-making. Voluntary associations not limited to the state may be empowered to debate ends and means alike, most notably perhaps regarding economic matters so that issues of investment, taxation, employment, and so on could be deliberated upon not only by politicians, economists, and captains of industry but also by labor unions and others with a stake in economic policy.

All of this is to be carried out with an eye toward the common good, although as we have mentioned, Dewey would always retain a form of individualism which he sought to bring into coherence with a brand of left politics that he continued to call liberal and which some have compared to guild socialism. Dewey's political works are quite clear about what he was opposing. An individualism premised on a conception of the human being as *Homo economicus* had not withstood the Hegelian critique, and in practice it had led to a capitalistic oligarchy which is the undoing of American democracy. At the same time he was more than a little wary of the varieties of socialist politics that he was observing in various nations of the world. The Russian experiment was a disaster which was following the formula of replacing one authoritarian state with another. The kind of Marxism that Soviet Russia and the Chinese Communist Party had adopted spoke the language of socialism while putting their societies on a road to tyranny. A more European democratic socialism held more promise, he believed, but any such conception would need to be squared with American individualism and culture, which for many will call to mind an elixir composed of equal parts of oil and water but for which Dewey held out considerable hope. Details were lacking if one wishes to see a larger picture, but he did indicate, at least in outline form, what such a model would contain and some of its underlying principles. An American liberal-socialist democracy (not his term) approximates a modern form of guild socialism whose British advocates at the time include the aforementioned Green, Hobhouse, and Hobson as well as writers like Arthur Penty, R. H. Tawney, G. D. H. Cole, and Bertrand Russell. The appeal of the guild model was that it was less oligarchical than both capitalism and authoritarian socialism and placed political and economic decision-making in the hands of a larger social body which would be less inclined toward centralization, factionalism, economic egoism, and factory production. This form of socialism, as Gary Bullert explains,

> constituted an ideal, long-range model toward which piecemeal reforms and voluntary organizations would be directed. Guild

socialism avoided the evils of governmental centralization and bureaucracy, while stressing social cooperation and participation. One could have voluntary planning without dictatorship. . . . During the Great Depression, Dewey demanded specific reforms that would temporarily increase state activity. Even during this statist period, he would espouse the ideal of local community and voluntary groups.[24]

The alliance of state power and big business needed to be broken and without ushering in a new collectivism, which would again amount to substituting one oligarchy for another.

His political stance underwent a degree of evolution over the course of his career and in response to events that importantly included the depression of the 1930s and Franklin D. Roosevelt's resulting New Deal. One might expect a left-leaning liberal at the time to have endorsed the New Deal with some enthusiasm, but Dewey would remain unsatisfied with measures that seemed to him not to go far enough in breaking the business-state alliance just alluded to. Some sort of mixed economy seemed to him the best alternative—not the abolition of capitalism nor its complete antithesis but an intermediate position of which Roosevelt's measures provided an inadequate approximation. The new welfare state amounted to capitalism plus a safety net and did not fundamentally alter American democracy in the manner Dewey desired, although again exactly what kind of rapprochement between liberalism and socialism he wished to see would remain sketchy. Robert Westbrook remarks, "By the end of the twenties John Dewey would admit, if pressed, that he was a socialist, for he was convinced that democracy required an end to private control of the commanding heights of the means of production." At the same time, "He avoided the word 'socialism' if he could, and when he could not he was careful to discriminate between his own peculiar socialist vision and the one he identified with the common usage of the word, between 'liberal' or 'democratic' socialism and authoritarian, bureaucratic, or, as he most often characterized it, 'state' socialism." Be that as it may, "his thinking remained bedeviled by the lack of a clear program of action," hovering between two sets of positions—oligarchies of both the right and the left—to which he was equally and adamantly opposed.[25] A non-state, non-centralized, non-bureaucratic, non-welfare, and non-collectivist socialism was perhaps more clear in articulating what it was not than what it was, but the details of such a program depended in some degree on the outcome of democratic inquiries that had yet to happen.

Political theory in the spirit of apriorism was never Dewey's project but was characteristic of the sort of ideologies that he opposed for the reason that a just political order is not an outcome of blackboard reasoning alone but is forever contingent on local factors that include customs and tradition as well as the moral values and attitudes that prevail in a given community. Democracy does not ride roughshod over this ground but emerges from it, as it had emerged in America from the conditions of eighteenth-century life. His notions of "the public" and "the great community" signified a social body that is unified by a great many forms of communication and by social bonds of a largely traditional kind (he mentions as examples "the family, church and neighborhood"). A salient fact of modern life is the loosening and decline of such bonds, the consequences of which Dewey believed to be ubiquitous and tragic. The ground of a democracy that is more than a set of institutions but an ethos and a way of life is "face-to-face communities" and the "settled relationships" that are found there. *The Public and Its Problems* is not a conservative work, but it would find its author reflecting that

[t]hat happiness which is full of content and peace is found only in enduring ties with others, which reach to such depths that they go below the surface of conscious experience to form its undisturbed foundation. No one knows how much of the frothy excitement of life, of mania for motion, of fretful discontent, of need for artificial stimulation, is the expression of frantic search for something to fill the void caused by the loosening of the bonds which hold persons together in immediate community of experience.[26]

What had become characteristic of large swaths of American life, he observed, is that with ever-increasing modernization and urbanization, the ties that bind us to one another had become external and mechanical, quasi-commercial and shallow, or otherwise short on meaning, and the effects—psychological, sociological, moral, and so on—of this loosening of relations were being felt in political life no less than various other dimensions of experience. No democracy can thrive in these conditions, and factionalism, enmity, and self-seeking are their natural consequences. What it requires is a wide combination of more traditional associative relations as well as an organizing principle that is capable of unifying the persons and collectivities that comprise it into an integrated public. This unifying condition is democratic communication itself and a way of life that is organized around both it and the social ties that were rapidly disappearing. "The significant thing," he elsewhere remarked, "is that the loyalties which once held individuals, which gave them support, direction and unity of outlook on life, have well-nigh disappeared. In consequence, individuals are confused and bewildered," and the difficulty this would pose for a democratic community may well be unsolvable.[27] Democracy is a plant that grows in a particular soil, and while no philosopher can proffer a formula for how the kind of associative ties he was speaking of might be conserved or restored, it may be noted that relations of this order are a sine qua non of what he called "a democratic effective Public."[28]

Dewey's Hegelianism must be kept in mind here. A new liberalism requires as a condition of possibility what Hegel termed *Sittlichkeit* or a general way of life that is organized around the ethical bonds and loyalties to which Dewey was alluding. Family, church, labor and professional organizations, civil society groups, and friends and neighbors interacting with some view toward the common good is the ground from which a community of democratic inquiry might emerge, but the fragility of such a community must be emphasized. Imagine an ecosystem: one finds a spontaneously emergent and dynamic network of organisms, relations, forces, and environmental conditions interacting with unlimited complexity and seeming stability at the same time that the whole is fragile and may be thrown into crisis through an erosion of a few of its basic elements or the sudden introduction of factors that tend toward its destabilization. A human community is like this, and variously thrives or declines as the elements that comprise it and the larger ethos that holds them together fare well or badly. The point he was making may appear conservative to a contemporary audience, but it is that a liberal democracy stands or falls on a form of ethical life that was in decline a century ago (and has undoubtedly continued on that trajectory ever since). The loss of tradition and customary social ties is worrisome not only for their own sake but for the sake of the political society that directly depends upon them, and one finds Dewey remarking upon this periodically throughout his career. The "great community" requires from the individual a free application of one's talents toward some public-spirited cause or other and from the collectivity a respect for individual freedom, a dynamism of personality and community that is mutually nourishing and neither egoistic nor collectivistic. It requires as well that the scale of social life not become so large as to make authentic association impossible. As he put it, "In its deepest and richest sense a community must always remain a matter of face-to-face intercourse. This is why the family and neighborhood, with all their deficiencies, have always been the chief agencies of nurture, the means by which dispositions are stably formed and ideas acquired which laid hold on the roots of character."[29]

Certain of Dewey's nineteenth-century New England sensibilities are surely apparent in passages of this kind, and they go to the root of the conception of liberal democracy that he sought to articulate. It was no nostalgic return to some real or imagined past that he was gesturing toward but an alternative to certain currents of modern life about which this otherwise progressive optimist was deeply worried. One characteristic passage in an essay from 1928 finds him remarking,

> If one looks at the overt and outer phenomena, at what I may call the public and official, the externally organized, side of our life, my own feeling about it would be one of discouragement. We seem to find everywhere a hardness, a tightness, a clamping down of the lid, a regimentation and standardization, a devotion to efficiency and prosperity of a mechanical and quantitative sort.[30]

Elsewhere he would speak in similarly critical terms of the "[e]xorbitant desire for uniformity of procedure and for prompt external results" as "the chief foes" of education, while in an economic context he remarked, "Quantification, mechanization and standardization: these are then the marks of the Americanization that is conquering the world. They have their good side; external conditions and the standard of living are undoubtedly improved. But their effects are not limited to these matters; they have invaded mind and character, and subdued the soul to their own dye."[31] Many of the watchwords of his time—modernization, standardization, normalization, urbanization, regimentation—were suggestive of a new uniformity of thought and behavior that was resolutely anti-individual and antithetical to a democratic way of life. Cultural bankruptcy is the consequence of an exclusive valorization of external utilities and shallow amusements which he was observing throughout American life. Popular diversions and entertainment seemed to him symptomatic of an increasingly rootless civilization, while the business of creating democratic community was delegated to political officeholders whose exclusive concern was winning elections. All told, it was not a sunny prognosis, and the right and the left were both implicated in what had gone wrong.

Of the left, Dewey took the view that anti-capitalist and anti-individualist sentiments had too often inclined its adherents toward an ideological stance that was lacking epistemic humility, and Marxism was the chief culprit. Dialectical materialism's claim to scientificity reflected nineteenth-century scientific notions that no longer held up, and quickly led to an authoritarianism that the Soviet experiment had made readily visible. By the early 1930s Dewey was violating a taboo in leftist circles by being openly critical of the Soviet Union and of its efforts to create a planned society which, having squeezed out any conception of autonomous individuality or authentic community, was no improvement over the oppressive state that preceded it. One form of tyrant had replaced another, now in the name of scientific modernity, while fascist Germany and Italy had adopted a similar logic on the far right. The antidote to the different forms of authoritarianism we see in the twentieth century, Dewey believed, lies outside of political ideology and in a view of knowledge that accentuates values of experimentation, finitude, and contingency. Political pragmatism undermines the ground on which all authoritarianism stands by eschewing the spirit of self-certainty and absolutism that is especially evident at the far ends of the left-right spectrum. The democrat must locate oneself somewhere proximal to the sane center, for it is from there that one can entertain contesting claims with an open mind along with one's fellow citizens. As we have seen, Dewey stood left of the center of the political spectrum of his time, but he was no ideologue and he was capable more than occasionally of drawing upon conservative ideas, depending on the issue and the circumstances. The America of his time was no fascist Germany or communist Russia, but its democratic way of life in his estimation faced active threats which issued in the main from much the same spirit of absolutism from which so much of the old world was suffering. As he expressed the point in *Freedom and Culture,* "The serious threat to our democracy is not the existence of foreign totalitarian states. It is the existence within our own personal attitudes and within our own institutions of conditions similar to those which have given a victory to external authority, discipline, uniformity and dependence upon The Leader in foreign countries. The battlefield is also accordingly here—within ourselves and our institutions," and primarily in the form of intellectual uniformity.[32] The standardization of public opinion that had been brought about through propaganda, inadequate educational institutions, and a rigid two-party system had become antithetical to the democracy he envisioned, while its ostensible defenders were drinking from the same well as its enemies abroad.

Some of the details of Dewey's political thought are clarified by looking at the activist work he engaged in over the course of his career and which complemented his more theoretical writings. A thorough analysis of this would require book-length treatment, but let us mention just a couple of the more important issues that occupied him in various political activities and shorter works written for a general audience, one regarding domestic politics and one foreign. Regarding the latter, Dewey lived through two world wars and was characteristically vocal on both. The experience of the first war convinced him of the need for international laws that would effectively forbid nations from conducting war under any and all circumstances. His participation in the "outlawry of war" movement occupied a good part of his energies in the aftermath of that war and through the 1920s, and he would oppose American involvement in the early part of the Second World War as well until the attack on Pearl Harbor. Unconditional pacifism—the unconditional in general— is not possible for a political experimentalist, as peace itself is not absolute but is one of many potentially conflicting values. Preventing the spread of totalitarianism is another value, and if military force was the only effective means of bringing this about, then it needed to be resorted to. His stance in both wars was not doctrinaire but evolved with the circumstances.

In domestic politics, Dewey would lose confidence in the two-party system and became enamored with the idea of a third party whose platform would tend to the left of both established parties. The economic realities of the thirties had made clear, in his view, that the Democratic and Republican parties were equally incapable of reigning in the capitalist oligarchy and serving the interests of the American working and middle classes. Some creative rapprochement between liberals and socialists was needed, but the realities of organized politics made this an unrealizable aim and a source of frustration for Dewey till the end of his days. As Westbrook writes, "Dewey's activism slowed in the forties, yet he remained remarkably involved in practical politics for a man approaching ninety. He continued to push nationally and in New York for a radical third party committed to democratic socialism, although by the end of the decade his political prognostications became increasingly wistful."[33]

The conditions of a more perfect democracy as he saw it crucially bear upon the way of life that prevails in a given nation at a given time and especially the mode of communication that is possible there.

The kind of experimental inquiry that holds center stage in several branches of his philosophy lay somewhat off in the distance in the real world of democratic politics, although he remained an optimist that the general citizenry of Western constitutional democracies was more than capable of governing themselves in the fashion for which he called and that the difficulties posed by economic egoism, factionalism, and so on, were solvable problems provided that certain social conditions were in place. The latter include the condition of our educational institutions, and it is to this that we now turn.

Notes

1 Dewey, *The Public and Its Problems*, LW 2 (1927), 264.

2 Dewey, *Freedom and Culture*, LW 13 (1939), 87.

3 Dewey, *Liberalism and Social Action*, LW 11 (1935), 20.

4 Dewey, *Freedom and Culture*, LW 13 (1939), 155.

5 Dewey, *The Public and Its Problems*, LW 2 (1927), 328–9.

6 Dewey, *The Public and Its Problems*, LW 2 (1927), 328.

7 Dewey, *Freedom and Culture*, LW 13 (1939), 153.

8 Dewey, *Liberalism and Social Action*, LW 11 (1935), 37.

9 Dewey, *Ethics*, LW 7 (1932), 361.

10 Dewey, *Liberalism and Social Action*, LW 11 (1935), 35–6. A few pages prior to this, Dewey would write: "I am one who believes that we need more, not fewer, 'rugged individuals' and it is in the name of rugged individualism that I challenged the argument. Instead of independence, there exists parasitical dependence on a wide scale—witness the present need for the exercise of charity, private and public, on a vast scale." "The argument" he was challenging is rugged individualism in its classical form together with its "unceasing glorification of the virtues of initiative, independence, choice and responsibility, virtues that centre in and proceed from individuals as such." LW 11 (1935), 29.

11 Dewey, *Liberalism and Social Action*, LW 11 (1935), 27.

12 Dewey, *Liberalism and Social Action*, LW 11 (1935), 31.

13 Dewey, *Ethics*, LW 7 (1932), 219.

14 Dewey, *Freedom and Culture*, LW 13 (1939), 142.

15 Dewey, *Individualism, Old and New*, LW 5 (1929), 81, 109.

16 Dewey, *Ethics*, LW 7 (1932), 348–9.

17 Dewey, *Freedom and Culture*, LW 13 (1939), 137.

18 Dewey, *Liberalism and Social Action*, LW 11 (1935), 41.

19 Dewey, *Liberalism and Social Action*, LW 11 (1935), 44, 21.

20 Dewey, "The Prospects of the Liberal College," MW 15 (1924), 203.

21 Dewey, *How We Think*, LW 8 (1933), 335.

22 Dewey, *Ethics*, LW 7 (1932), 358, 362.

23 Dewey, *Liberalism and Social Action*, LW 11 (1935), 48.

24 Gary Bullert, *The Politics of John Dewey* (Buffalo: Prometheus Books, 1983), 25–6.

25 Robert B. Westbrook, *John Dewey and American Democracy* (Ithaca: Cornell University Press, 1991), 429, 439.

26 Dewey, *The Public and Its Problems*, LW 2 (1927), 368–9. In the same book he would write, "The invasion of the community by the new and relatively impersonal and mechanical modes of combined human behavior is the outstanding fact of modern life." LW 2 (1927), 296.

27 Dewey, *Individualism, Old and New*, LW 5 (1929), 66.

28 Dewey, *The Public and Its Problems*, LW 2 (1927), 333.

29 Dewey, *The Public and Its Problems*, LW 2 (1927), 367.

30 Dewey, "A Critique of American Civilization," LW 3 (1928), 134.

31 Dewey, *Democracy and Education*, MW 9 (1916), 182. Dewey, *Individualism, Old and New*, LW 5 (1929), 52.

32 Dewey, *Freedom and Culture*, LW 13 (1939), 98.

33 Westbrook, *John Dewey and American Democracy*, 461.

6

Philosophy of Education

It is not unusual for social reformers, in Dewey's time or our own, to look to education as a remedy for whatever conditions afflict, or are believed to afflict, the times or as a pathway to whatever political aims they wish to bring about, and Dewey's contribution to the theory of education may be understood at least partly in this light. *Democracy and Education* is not only the title of the foremost of several treatises he would publish in this field but a logical pairing, and his numerous contributions to educational theory would make constant reference to democracy in his distinctive understanding of the term. A precondition of a viable democratic order is an educated citizenry—in itself not an original claim, but Dewey's interpretation of the claim and its implications would account for a major portion of his philosophical output through several books and scores of essays as well as a good part of his activist work, most notably at the famous Laboratory School at the University of Chicago which Dewey established in 1896. Dewey himself received a conventional precollege education and about as fine a postsecondary education as was available in latter-nineteenth-century America, and his experience led him to lament the condition in which public schools in particular found themselves by century's end. His criticisms were numerous, and we shall mention the more central ones through the course of this chapter in order to contrast his own proposals with the traditional approaches of which he became America's preeminent critic.

Let us begin with a brief overview of his critique of standard educational methods as they were commonly practiced in America and a great many countries and to some extent remain mainstream in the schools of our own time. The traditional classroom typically grouped students by age, sat them in individual desks arranged in rows and facing the teacher at the head of the class, was orderly and often quiet, and the children were to listen while the teacher offered whole-class instruction in standard subjects. Emphasis was placed upon tests, rote learning, and grades while the students' learning in general was regarded as a preparation for later life and in particular for their eventual entry into the workforce. A fair amount of discipline was believed to be a necessary way of dealing both with behavioral issues and with any deficits in interest and motivation which were not infrequent accompaniments of this model. Dewey would fault such an arrangement on a number of grounds but principally for its disconnection from students' experience and interests, its sterility and conventionalism, its excessive emphasis upon information retention, and the passivity of the students. The central business of all education, he maintained, is thinking, and this is learned not by cramming in as much information as the mind will more or less unwillingly absorb but by practicing the art in question. One learns X by doing X and in no other way, but when thinking takes a back seat to information retention—much of which is short term—little is learned while obstacles are placed in the path of inquiry.

By this point it will come as no surprise that experimental inquiry lies at the center of Dewey's philosophy of education, as it has been in each of the preceding chapters. This is the heart and soul of all education and particularly the sort of education for which a democratic way of life calls. The traditional educational model is suited to a social order that is either autocratic or aristocratic in that it prepares the young to take their place in a society whose salient features are obedience and old-world classism. What a school is, on Dewey's view, is a nascent community in which the same practices and capacities that a democracy elicits are learned at an elementary level. It is no cloister but "a special environment" that is "framed with express reference to influencing the mental and moral disposition of their members."[1] The various disciplines ought not be regarded by the students as "academic" in a colloquial sense but as arising from their own experience and from the shared experience of a particular form of social life, while "the school itself shall be made a genuine form of active community life, instead of a place set apart in which to learn lessons."[2]

Before turning to details, it is important to recall the larger conception of the theory/practice relation that pragmatism proposes. A philosophical theory of education, or of anything, for Dewey is the antithesis of a castle in the air; it is a set of hypotheses that attempts to clarify what is already going on in our practices and to critique and often redirect our actions in light of a given practice's internal logic and aims. Education does not need to be supplied with theoretically generated ends as it already contains several which the philosopher must render explicit. Abstract theorizing takes as its starting point not "what education *should* be," in the sense of what values conceived outside of the educative process itself (an ideology, doctrine, tradition, etc.) ought to be imposed upon it, but "what actually takes place when education really occurs."[3] As he would express this important principle in *Democracy and Education*, "In our search for aims in education, we are not concerned, therefore, with finding an end outside of the educative process to which education is subordinate. Our whole conception forbids. We are rather concerned with the contrast which exists when aims belong within the process in which they operate and when they are set up from without."[4] Theory and practice stand in a dialectical, not hierarchical, relation wherein the former takes the latter as its point of departure and ultimately returns to it and endeavors to enhance it in light of a clarified understanding of what the practice itself is and what ends it serves. What results is a philosophy neither of liberal education, progressive education, nor conservative education but of education simpliciter, "with no qualifying adjectives prefixed."[5] A related point is that in addition to education being a practice with its own immanent logic it is also an art. The business of teaching and learning ought to incorporate whatever scientific knowledge is to be had regarding child psychology but a science itself it is not and nor is it capable of becoming one. Dewey did not inflate the distinction between art and science into a dichotomy, but nor did he dispense with it or hold out hope that education might be placed on the secure path of a science: "No conclusion of scientific research can be converted into an immediate rule of educational art. For there is no educational practice whatever which is not highly complex; that is to say, which does not contain many other conditions and factors than are included in the scientific finding."[6]

As mentioned, the concept of experimental inquiry is at the core of Dewey's theory of education. When students are presented with subject matter in any discipline which does not connect in any appreciable degree with their out-of-school experience, the prospect of learning beyond the stage of short-term retention is bleak indeed, and this was an important part of his critique of traditional schooling. The alternative is to present less and to inquire more. Learning is an activity, and as with any activity the student must develop a capacity for agency such that external direction is replaced with direction from within—not overnight, of course, but gradually over the course of the learning process. The student, even at a young age, is not a patient but an agent in the making, but to become this one must exercise some initiative both in choosing what subject matters one is going to investigate and then in engaging in free inquiry. At the postsecondary level this may be readily seen: one arrives at the university, let us say, with a relatively serious interest in politics or economics and sets about selecting a degree program and courses, followed by particular assignments, all of which are occasions for the student to inquire along with their professors and peers into the specifics of that field of knowledge. Books are read, essays are written, and so on, with an eye to what is to be discovered and what arguments formulated and ideas critiqued, while whatever information is gained is a consequence of student-led inquiry. In the lower grades, the same principle applies on a more elementary level: again the students are inquiring with their teachers into a given subject matter and are not simply presented with a ready-made curriculum which they must absorb and retain long enough to pass an examination. The students are called upon to show initiative both in selecting topics of inquiry and subsequently carrying it out under an educator's tutelage.

The classroom as he conceived it is designed not on the old model but more along the lines of a laboratory, a workshop, or a traditional home. Neither of these is particularly quiet or well ordered from the point of view of the outsider, and indeed many a visitor to "the Dewey school" in Chicago noted the boisterousness of the students as they would go about performing laboratory experiments or conversing about some project or shared undertaking. The student was to be actively engaged in learning, and far less in the customary manner of being on the receiving end of information being directed at them by the teacher than in the way one gets caught up in an activity in which one takes an unforced interest. As he would write in an early work, "The child comes to school to *do*; to cook, to sew, to work with wood and tools in simple constructive acts; within and about these acts cluster the studies—writing, reading, arithmetic, etc."[7] Learning is an activity, and if cooking or sewing does not appear especially educative it is likely because we are regarding the activity in isolation rather than, as Dewey urged, as a prelude to what we are more likely to recognize as an academic subject matter. Consider an elementary example: a boy arrives in a seventh-grade classroom with a fervent interest in baseball. Baseball is not Shakespeare, nor is it mathematics, history, or any other conventional subject which one would expect a formal education to impart. It has no place in a school, except perhaps in the playground during free time or at most during gym class—so our traditionalist will suppose. Dewey's point is not that baseball is inherently educative (nothing, in his view, is inherently educative) but that it may lead into any number of inquiries which such a student could undertake, whether it be into statistics, the history of the game, its relevance to American culture, the economics or mathematics of sports, physiology, and biology, or any line of questioning which could arise directly or indirectly from an interest in this game. By the same token, cooking, sewing, or any similar household activity may serve as an initiation into physics, chemistry, history, economics, and so on provided that students are permitted and expected to inquire into some line of questioning that stems in an organic way from such activities.

A crucial factor in all educational activity is the environment in which it takes place, and Dewey would make this a central theme in his work in this field. Again using the model of the laboratory, workshop, or home, "a certain atmosphere of informality" is to be preferred "because experience has proved that formalization is hostile to genuine mental activity and to sincere emotional expression and growth."[8] Too much formality and externally imposed structure inhibit the free exercise of the mind—which is not a call to fly to the opposite extreme (a point to which we shall return) but an endorsement of an educational environment in which relatively free and self-directed forms of activity may be carried out under the supervision of the teacher. There are environments that are natural attendants of certain kinds of experience in that they make possible and sustain a particular form of activity, and in the case of education an appropriate "learning environment" accomplishes a fair amount of work in setting the stage for intellectual and experiential growth. A traditional workshop is an appropriate setting for various forms of woodworking and any cognate activities while a scientist's lab again affords the conditions that make it possible to pursue certain forms of experimentation, and both are suited to the kind of school Dewey was recommending. Additionally, "The life of the child would extend out of doors to the garden, surrounding fields, and forests. He would have his excursions, his walks and talks, in which the larger world out of doors would open to him."[9] All of this constitutes an effective educational environment provided it creates the conditions that promote the ready exchange of ideas and a continual growth in experience.

The role of the educator on this view is to be neither the principal driver of the learning process nor an ineffectual bystander but, in keeping with the etymology of the word, to affect a "drawing out" and a "leading forth" of the students from where they are to where they might be. To lead in this sense is not to cause or drag along but to guide in light of the teacher's knowledge of the subject matter and in a horse to water fashion. The student learns far more "through the overflow of its own activities" than by having information plastered on by an external authority, and this psychological truth must be borne in mind by teachers who can be overly eager to arrive at the conclusion of a process that is naturally accumulative and unhurried.[10] Gardeners know that a steady, all-day rain is better than a downpour, and the educational counterpart to this is that knowledge penetrates the student's consciousness and leads to growth when it accumulates in a slow and steady way, and also when the student is the primary agent. "The teacher," in his view, "loses the position of external boss or dictator but takes on that of leader of group activities."[11] Dewey's conservative critics quickly inferred that the teacher either drops out of the picture or "leads" in the sense of standing on the sidelines while occasionally injecting a bit of information, while his actual view was nothing of the kind. A "leader of group activities," let us say in a class on music, has a certain amount of musical knowledge and in light of this knows where a particular activity is likely to lead, not merely in an immediate sense but in future years. A given student is holding an instrument in an incorrect way and if left to their own devices will not gain any facility with the instrument if they continue to hold it in whatever way they please. The student requires correction, and this is a small example of what "leading" involves. The teacher might also suggest a particular song that the students might learn to play, and where the selection is likely to be based on the students' aesthetic preferences and the level of technical difficulty it requires. Leading here further involves a coordinating of who plays what and a conducting of the group so that what results is not uncoordinated noise but something resembling music. The teacher organizes, directs, suggests, informs, and corrects but does not dominate the scene. Its "direction is but *re*-direction" in that "it shifts the activities already going on into another channel." Its leading is more an overseeing and a coaching than a commanding. The music class in which the teacher is the general and the students are privates might succeed in achieving some short-term goals, but in the long run it is likely to prove an obstacle to future learning in this area. A teenage garage band has no general and typically affords more fertile ground for this kind of activity than a traditional music classroom, that is, unless we assume in the latter case that the students already have a relatively advanced interest in what the teacher has to impart. In that case, the educator—in the university, let us say—may need to spend considerable time delivering information (lecturing) in the customary sense, although even here information is not yet knowledge and too much of it "swamps thinking."[12] The mind that is overfull of ill-digested information is not able to do anything with it but retain it for usually short periods of time before jettisoning the lot, as many of us can testify to when looking back on our high school days. How much of that material is retained and available for intelligent use a decade or two later? If the answer is not a lot, the cause is likely that a pre-packaged curriculum was uploaded into the short-term memory and then forgotten upon the conclusion of a given course. The experience of many a student in a traditional school, Dewey noted, is that the classroom is an alien environment in which information of no obvious relation to one's experience must be ingested in the largest possible quantity as an end in itself while occasions to reflect upon or otherwise do something inventive with it are few.

The concept of experience is central to Dewey's position here again. The "Copernican revolution" for which he called recenters education around the students' own experience rather than the teacher or the curriculum alone. The basis for this move is the consideration that human beings from the moment they are born have experiences of myriad kinds and incessantly negotiate their way through the world in ways that result in learning, while when they arrive at school the lion's share of this is put aside as experience and education are for all intents and purposes divorced. Learning is a natural accompaniment of a great deal of the student's out-of-school experience, yet a common phenomenon finds a child's mind possessing a voracious appetite for certain forms of extracurricular learning while wholly unmotivated with respect to school subjects. What has gone wrong is that the educational system has created a "gap in kind (as distinct from degree) between the child's experience and the various forms of subject-matter that make up the course of study," Dewey's remedy to which is as follows:

> From the side of the child, it is a question of seeing how his experience already contains within itself elements—facts and truths—of just the same sort as those entering into the formulated study; and, what is of more importance, of how it contains within itself the attitudes, the motives, and the interests which have operated in developing and organizing the subject-matter to the plane which it now occupies. From the side of the studies, it is a question of interpreting them as outgrowths of forces operating in the child's life, and of discovering the steps that intervene between the child's present experience and their richer maturity.[13]

The starting point in education, both formal and informal, is the experience and existing interests of the students, regardless of age or educational level. These are the initial ingredients with which the teacher has to work, and their task is not merely to indulge for their own sake interests which may be quite childish but to enlist them as a starting point of an inquiry that may be anticipated to lead toward a higher (more general, theoretical, or abstract) form of knowledge. The common trajectory of such experience is from the particular to the universal, from the practical to the theoretical, and from the familiar to the unfamiliar, and the crucial point for Dewey is that should the teacher begin with the latter in each of these pairings then, especially in the case of children, a motivational deficit is a predictable result. The perennial question of students, "Why do we need to know this?," demands to be answered in a way that they themselves can feel the force of, and "Because you will need it some day" will not do. The latter is not motivational, particularly for the very young, and if we wish students to put in the labor that real learning involves, the student must perceive some vital connection between what they are studying and their extracurricular life.

Dewey was not asserting either that all out-of-school experience is educationally worthwhile or to an equal degree or that students in traditional schools did not have experiences. They clearly did, however, the problem is the nature and quality of those experiences and their disconnection from ordinary life. There are educative and miseducative experiences and distinguishing between them bears upon nothing inherent to the experiences themselves but upon that to which they lead. Simplifying somewhat, an experience of mathematics, baseball, or anything in between is miseducative if it blocks the path of future experience, and it is educationally worthwhile under the opposite condition. Human experience is organic in the sense that it contains dimensions that are discrete but interrelated; one thing within it leads to another, moves and grows beyond itself into some other avenue, and relates in complex ways with an array of other experiences. Education aims to foster ongoing and ultimately lifelong experiential growth and fails when it confines experience within wholly predetermined avenues or inhibits it entirely. "An experience," as he noted, "may be such as to engender callousness; it may produce lack of sensitivity and of responsiveness. Then the possibilities of having richer experience in the future are restricted."[14] It may create enervating routine, aimlessness, or habits of an excessively "bookish" sort, if we intend by this a knowledge that does not relate in some meaningful way to other dimensions of our experience. In saying this he was not opposing areas of study that are at some remove from the everyday—he was a philosopher after all—but educational approaches that build castles in the air or that regard the school as an island cut off from the larger society.

In general, the information and experiences that are to be had in any educational setting must accord with and have their basis in the "indirect education" that characterizes so much of the student's extracurricular experience, where learning so often comes readily and naturally.[15] Dewey in *Democracy and Education* would thus offer a concise and "technical definition of education" as follows: "It is that reconstruction or reorganization of experience which adds to the meaning of experience, and which increases ability to direct the course of subsequent experience."[16] It does not indulge but enlists the students' existing interests as a starting point of intellectual investigation for the simple reason that "they are all there is, so to speak, to the child; they are all the teacher has to appeal to; they are the starting points, the initiatives, the working machinery." He immediately added that such interests are not ends in themselves but starting points only: "The significance of interest is in what *it leads to*; to new experiences it makes possible, the new powers it tends to form."[17] Many a critic took Dewey to task for, as they supposed, advocating that students pass the school day more or less amusing themselves in mindless pursuits—a charge that is quickly defused by actually reading his books, as many evidently elected not to do.[18] To utilize a student's interest in much of anything, as he repeatedly clarified, is not to indulge it or treat it as an end in itself but to harness and redirect it toward something that is educationally worthwhile and in which the student can take an unforced interest owing to its organic connection with that in which they are already interested. We mentioned the example of baseball; now let us consider a more abstract example. Philosophy is not a subject in which most teenagers are interested, or not at any rate when it is presented as so many abstract and technical issues found in a textbook. To all appearances it can resemble an alien planet the route to which is forbidding and the point of which is all but impossible to see. Properly introduced, it is the very opposite of this but an activity that the students themselves are already engaged in and vitally concerned with yet without realizing it. In a time when "cancel culture" and "deplatforming" are a commonplace topic of conversation, there is no need for the teacher of philosophy to "make it interesting" when one relates the story of the gadfly of Athens, nor need one "make interesting" the topic of anxiety or suffering, death, justice, or education itself. Most students are already interested in philosophical questions and need only be invited not to a museum tour in the history of ideas but to a conversation that bears upon a vital aspect of their lives and which opens onto any number of disciplines in which they may previously have had no interest. One is not born with an interest in abstruse subjects but comes to them, if at all, by the natural route that is following a chain of interests which usually proceeds from the particular to the abstract and the narrow to the broad.

The educational values of broadening horizons and opening oneself to experience are not unique to Dewey but are deeply rooted in the *Bildung* tradition in post-Hegelian thought, and his own Hegelianism is evident in this area of his work no less than in his ontology. Dewey did not employ the term *Bildung*, but the conception of education as an encompassing and gradual formation of the person in the direction of greater sophistication and critical participation in one's culture is fundamentally Hegelian, as he was undoubtedly aware, and it emerges from his earliest to his latest work in educational thought in the idea of growth. As the aim of growth in general is more growth, the ultimate aim of education is more education in the sense of a learning from experience that does not come to an end upon graduating from a particular course of study and indeed does not end at all. To speak of education as growth entails first that it is an end in itself over and above being valuable as a means of preparation for later life or for an economic vocation. Dewey was not about to deny the instrumental value of a good education; it has indeed long prepared the young to enter the workforce and to take their place in the larger life of their society, and this is a part of its value. His point was that this is not the whole of it, but that education also possesses an inherent value which is largely unseen. Consider the notion of preparation: its meaning lies in nothing within itself but in that for which we are getting ready, and it is the future that is valued at the expense of the present. As children have little regard for the future, teachers customarily find it necessary to compel their charges to take up the tasks they are meant to be learning. The "good student" is compliant in this while the problem student remains occupied with present distractions and is given to procrastination, which itself involves an absorption in the present moment at the expense of the future. Effective preparation, Dewey noted, is not this but almost the reverse: when a present experience or activity is properly undertaken, one extracts from it everything that is capable of being extracted, and as an important but secondary consequence, one creates the conditions that enable one to deal with what comes next. If a hockey coach wishes to prepare a promising sixteen-year-old for a career in the National Hockey League, he focuses the athlete not on the Stanley Cup but on the task at hand. It is the present game that demands full attention and the actions one must perform in order to win it. Only when we live through this fully do we prepare ourselves bit by bit for the future, and the same may be said of any academic subject matter. The often powerful motivation that attends present experience and present interests must be utilized by the teacher in slowly but surely leading the student from where they are to some more recognizably "academic" place. As he wrote, "To get ready for something, one knows not what nor why, is to throw away the leverage that exists, and to seek for motive power in a vague chance."[19] The vague chance is that the student is either compliant with whatever the teacher asks or is already interested in the lesson one is imparting, and it is not something on which the teacher can rely.

Effective preparation itself, then, is less future-oriented than we often imagine, while Dewey's larger point is that the true purpose of education transcends this and lies in the concept of growth. It is the nature of any growing thing that in order to reach a future stage of development the organism must first experience in full some earlier and less mature stage and for its own sake. Adolescence is not a mere staging ground for adulthood but a period of life that is meaningful in its own terms, and it is only when such meanings are experienced in whatever richness they offer that we are made ready for more mature pursuits in a process that continues throughout life. The learning process is its own goal, in contrast both with the traditional notion of education as a mere preparation for later, especially economic, life and with more current "outcomes-based" approaches where instrumentalism reigns once again. The indications of such growth are experiential continuity and interaction. By the former Dewey was referring to the way in which one thing in our experience leads to another and is not atomistic. Educationally worthwhile experiences are those that endure over time and build upon each other, for instance, in the formation of habits. One does not read Shakespeare without the ground having been prepared by a habit and a love of reading for its own sake, which if it has been acquired at all undoubtedly began with less sophisticated material and which has led one gradually to this stage. Experiential continuity can lead in any number of directions, for both good and ill; intellectual growth is but one of them, but when a regularity and consistency of experience is wedded to a kind of knowledge that is worth having, what comes of it is a momentum in which learning leads to more learning. "Every experience is a moving force" and "can be judged only on the ground of what it moves toward and into," be it toward learning about a more advanced field of knowledge or toward a mental habit that blocks the road of inquiry.[20] A particular form of growth is judged from an educational standpoint on whether it is or is not conducive to more growth of some desirable kind. Part of the educator's role, accordingly, is to distinguish those experiences that are likely to be fruitful in this sense from those that either lead nowhere or that lead to a bad end.

Experiential interaction connotes an integration or a hanging together of the different facets of experience into some coherent configuration. It is the nature of mature experience to display not only continuity from one course of inquiry or activity to the next but also an interaction between conditions both external and internal to the individual which comprise a given situation. "Any normal experience," as Dewey expressed it, "is an interplay of these two sets of conditions," that is, of the "objective" conditions that belong to an educational situation and the conditions that are "internal" to the mental life of the inquirer. If traditional educational methods erred in ignoring the importance of conditions internal to the individual student, or "what he is at a given time," progressives made the opposite error of ignoring objective conditions.[21] The two principles of continuity and interaction are not altogether separate in meaning and still less so in their applications since both refer to the essential connectedness of human experience and speak against the experiential atomism of traditional British empiricism. If experience is experimental then there is a flexible give and take between the inquirers themselves and the situation that is to be inquired into, and it is the combination of these two principles that marks an experience as properly educative. When a student's various experiences at school are continuous and integrated in the general manner he recommended and not fragmented or disconnected from extracurricular life, there is a natural momentum that pulls the student along in the direction of more learning. Their own interests can have an addictive quality and act as a powerful motivator in driving the learning process in a way that involves a tremendous output of effort while at the best of times appearing effortless. Think of the high school student of today who may be lackluster in their studies yet who cannot put down every volume of the *Harry Potter* series. This common phenomenon is but one illustration of the falsity of the interest versus effort opposition which remains deeply rooted in conventional thinking about education. The old idea that learning requires enormous effort in matters in which one is unlikely to be interested and that externally imposed discipline must be introduced as a motivating force Dewey rejected as yet another dichotomy which is based on a misunderstanding. Students indeed must put their back into their education or nothing will come of it, but to say this does not amount to an endorsement of effort over interest, discipline over freedom, or the stick over the carrot. The *Harry Potter* reader is likely (far more likely than the non-reader) to move on to other works of literature that are more usually regarded as educationally important and with little or no stick involved, as can be said of any popular gateway to higher learning. An overemphasis on effort and an underappreciation of existing interests tends to produce students who are externally directed and skilled in the art of feigning interest in matters they find lifeless and which they are sure to abandon at the first opportunity. For long- or even short-term learning to happen, the mind must pay attention—to the right things, in the right way, and for the right period of time—and the act of directing attention is nothing as simple as following a teacher's command. It involves pursuing an interest, and without this factor a motivational deficit is a predictable and permanent problem. No magic on the teacher's part can resolve this, and discipline beyond what the work itself requires is no solution if our aim is to produce students with an appetite for future learning. Such order as exists in the classroom properly reflects not the will of the teacher alone but that which is conducive to intelligent inquiry; "there is," he pointed out, "a certain disorder in any busy workshop," but it is the disorder not of aimless amusement but of purposive and cooperative activity.[22] Dewey was aware of the criticism that his own Laboratory School and later progressive schools appeared somewhat anarchic, and his reply was that productive work that involves some level of cooperation on a common task is not likely to be altogether stationary and silent, and regardless of their age.

As an educational philosopher, Dewey's focus was on process over outcomes, from which it does not follow that he cared little about or gave little thought to outcomes, for indeed he did. The way to bring about optimal results is by focusing not on results themselves—a way of thinking that typically lands one in some form of instrumentalism— but on the educational process and the learning environment, just as a gardener who in springtime dwells on the harvest is going to have a bad harvest. Dewey did, however, have a conception of what educational success and failure look like, and he articulated this by identifying particular intellectual virtues and vices which are less outcomes in the usual sense than indications of whether the process as a whole has been relatively successful. Let us begin with the vices. These are several and include some of the usual signs of unsuccess that educators have long identified, from low knowledge retention to listlessness, incuriosity, and closed-mindedness. He extended the list, however, to include self-certainty, overspecialization, the narrow or rigid mind, impatience, indiscipline, shallowness, excessive conventionality, a weak will, gullibility, and a propensity for academic cheating. Special attention was paid to the "antisocial spirit" of many an intellectual and others who might be regarded as educationally successful. Schools that "substitute a bookish, a pseudo-intellectual spirit for a social spirit" may succeed in instilling a facility with concepts and texts while failing to cultivate the larger sensibility that experimental and democratic inquiry demands.[23] The pedant who makes a show of his or her knowledge of the rules or technical details of this or that while giving no thought to their larger implications for human life is not an educational success, nor is the scientist who pays no mind to the possible ethical or social consequences of their research. The isolation of the school or university from the community, of a given line of research from cognate fields, and of individual thinking from some form of participation in social life are common vices against which Dewey warned. So as well is the kind of groupthink that is visible in all times and places in one form or another. A democratic way of life calls for a freedom of mind which is the antithesis of intellectual conformity; it requires that every citizen be thinking for himself or herself and in a public-spirited manner. As we saw in the last chapter, Dewey was a proponent of a new form of individualism that conflicted in no way with civic-mindedness or which amounted to a unity of individual creativity and social participation, and this political idea has an educational counterpart just as the old individualism of economic egoism had found its correlate in the bright but socially inept mind. Additional vices include the apathy that can ensue upon completing a given course of study (expressed in the often-heard phrase that one "has taken" a certain subject, with the implication that it is over and done with) and the related tendencies toward "undue reliance upon personal influence," including the influence of teachers, and "satisfying the teacher instead of the problem," where again the student's focus is on the teacher rather than the matter under discussion.[24]

Undue deference toward educators or the school itself and uncritical acceptance of any controversial doctrines they may wish to instill are additional intellectual vices about which Dewey warned. Education shades into indoctrination not when beliefs are passed down but when they are passed down in a way that prohibits or discourages inquiry. When the rational basis of any idea is off limits to discussion, the student becomes habituated to intellectual subordination and in later years is "the easy prey of skillful politicians and political machines" along with charlatans and propagandists.[25] The student is a democratic citizen and intellectual agent in the making, and neither is learned through subordination or by being force-fed ideas of whatever sort. It is not, for Dewey, off limits to teach the young patriotism, altruism, or any other value; what matters is the process by which this is accomplished, and all such beliefs, be they scientific, political, moral, religious, or anything else, are properly taught through inquiry and persuasion alone. One final vice that is worth noting is overspecialization. Dewey's warnings here bear upon the dangers that attend the narrowing of horizons that was setting in both in the workforce and in the universities of his day. Some amount of specialization no doubt yields utility, but the tendency toward excessive narrowness is a vice he believed to be evermore widespread. One characteristic remark reads:

> Specialization, in its measure and degree, means withdrawal. It means preoccupation with a comparatively remote field in relatively minute detail. I have no doubt that in the long run the method of specialization will justify itself, not only scientifically, but practically. But value in terms of ultimate results is no reason for disguising the immediate danger to courage, and the freedom that can come only from courage.

A couple of sentences later, he added: "The insidious conviction that certain matters of fundamental import to humanity are none of my concern because outside of my *Fach*, is likely to work more harm to genuine freedom of academic work than any fancied dread of interference from a moneyed benefactor."[26] The problem with the overspecialized mind is that it carries out its often impressive labors in disconnection from matters for which it carries consequences and to which it typically turns a blind eye, leaving unexamined whole areas of inquiry that forbid specialization while being "of fundamental import to humanity," or leaving such thinking to politicians or others who lack the capacity to carry it out effectively. He was alluding here to questions of a larger and more ambitious kind—of a kind that much of his own work took up—which resist being reduced to the kind of puzzles and minutiae that specialists often prefer, whether for reasons of manageability or failure of nerve. Inquiry, not only in philosophy, sometimes requires a free-spiritedness and a fearlessness that relatively narrow specialists are not known for, and when the world of scholarship in particular witnesses a "decline of liberality of mind" the consequences can be serious indeed and include the common phenomenon of "an authority in a particular field" who is "of more than usually poor judgment in matters not closely allied."[27]

The intellectual vices that Dewey singled out already indicate the kind of virtues he viewed as marks of educational success. The educated mind as he conceived it combines a broad horizon with a capacity for reflective depth, openness and creativity, flexibility and independence, patience and discipline, and an interdisciplinary and social spirit which is mindful of any larger implications of one's work beyond a narrow specialty. The ability and inclination to examine matters broadly and rigorously together with one's peers, a broad curiosity and capacity "[t]o be playful and serious at the same time," he described as "the ideal mental condition," and if the whole set of such virtues is not something one could expect every student to have mastered, these remain the closest Dewey would come to identifying outcomes of educational success.[28] The ultimate "learning outcome" (to use a contemporary and very un-Deweyan phrase) is the ability and need to continue learning throughout and also from life and not only within formal educational settings. The capacity and habit of learning from experience as an end in itself is indistinguishable from the growth that Dewey spoke of as education's highest aim. The successful student "learns to learn" in the sense that one is able to draw upon whatever experiences one has had and to apply knowledge to new situations in a process that does not end upon graduation.[29]

When education succeeds one becomes a lifelong student, not formally but in the sense of having cultivated habits of mind of the kind just alluded to and which one carries with one through life. One is able to inquire into problematic situations not limited to one's field of expertise and to converse with others about the issues that ail a democracy. While he would always emphasize the social spirit of intelligence, he maintained that "A person who has gained the power of reflective attention, the power to hold problems, questions, before the mind, *is*, in so far, intellectually speaking, *educated*. He has mental discipline—the power *of* the mind and *for* the mind."[30] Being educated in this sense encompasses sheer concentrative power together with discipline and judgment, a mind that is not at the mercy of whatever sophistry and propaganda a society offers up but is able to see through subterfuge, perceive the relations between things, and discriminate between what is relevant and irrelevant in a given situation. It is solution-oriented without opting for the hasty solution to a difficult problem and is able to accelerate and slow its operations according to the circumstances one encounters. Oftentimes, he remarked, the quality of our responses to problems depends upon "the plane upon which these occur," in the sense of whether we allow the circumstances in their richness to be absorbed to an appropriate depth before formulating a hypothesis or whether our response is based upon a superficial reading of the situation. Some problems are easily solved, but the ones that occasion serious inquiry demand an unhurried mind which is able to get to the root of a matter and to weigh competing considerations with the requisite thoroughness.

The educated mind is habituated toward self-control in the sense of being able to direct its thoughts in the right way toward the right things, exhibiting quick-wittedness when called for and patience and endurance when circumstances demand it. Often enough, he added, the "depth to which a sense of the problem, of the difficulty, sinks, determines the quality of the thinking that follows."[31]

We now see more clearly the vital connection between education and democracy. These two values are related not externally, as it were, in the sense that students must be indoctrinated with a controversial ideology, but internally: democracy and education are consubstantial in that they likewise participate in a way of life and an ethos of intelligence rather than coercion. A democratic order requires a democratic citizenship, and the latter are born citizens only in a superficial sense. They must be educated for it, where this means the antithesis of force-feeding a particular political doctrine. Students must be force-fed nothing at all if we are speaking of controversial ideas but rather initiated into forms of rational thought that make one invulnerable to this and any other kind of manipulation. Dewey clearly did not want teachers attempting to convince the intellectually immature of the superiority of one political creed over another. They are not to be partisan activists in the classroom, as many of his critics misunderstood him to mean, nor experts of any particular kind but fellow inquirers operating on the same epistemic level as the students. A teacher is but a more experienced student, one who can be expected to guide and inform the students' investigations without dominating them or manipulating the process to ensure some predetermined conclusion. A temptation every educator must resist is to instill whether overtly or covertly some controversial opinion of one's own into the minds of the students, be it political or any other. The aim of a democratic education is not to produce socialists, liberals, conservatives, or followers of any other philosophy; as we have noted, it is not "liberal education" but education simpliciter that Dewey was advocating and attempting to conceptualize, and at its heart is an experimental rationality that is the preserve of no political faction.

The distinction just alluded to between intelligence and coercion (ballots or bullets in a political context) may be as close as Dewey would ever come to a genuine dichotomy. In educational settings a necessary condition of the former is a relatively expansive freedom of inquiry, and it is for this reason that academic freedom is tantamount to a first principle of all genuine education. Without it, the whole business deteriorates into an indoctrination that primes students to go out into adult life vulnerable to manipulation by whatever half-baked ideas they encounter and ill-equipped to participate in a democratic way of life. Exactly what did he mean by academic freedom, for this is a concept with multiple connotations? In a work of 1929 he would write: "I don't like the phrase academic freedom because there really is nothing academic about freedom. Freedom of mind, freedom of thought, freedom of inquiry, freedom of discussion is education, and there is no education, no real education, without these elements of freedom. An attack upon what is called academic freedom is an attack upon intellectual integrity, and hence it is an attack upon the very idea of education and upon the possibility of education realizing its purpose. You can have training without mental freedom but you cannot get education."[32] "Academic freedom," then, is something of a tautology, and his dislike of the phrase does not indicate a rejection of what we commonly mean by it. Liberty of mind, thought, inquiry, and discussion is not an adjunct of education but an indispensable ingredient of it, and throughout Dewey's educational writings he would often repeat this point. A broad range of activities may be included under this general umbrella, from a child selecting which project they will undertake to a university professor writing a book and everything in between. Any and all hypotheses may be investigated, and where students are under no obligation to reach any predetermined conclusion. In Dewey's time this would include the teaching of evolution, where his position was that teachers must neither present this as incontrovertible fact nor forbid discussion of it but inquire with the students into an hypothesis in the usual manner of scientific investigation. A second illustration is afforded by Dewey's stance toward the Lusk laws of 1921–3 in the New York State that was his home after his move to Columbia University in 1904. These proposed laws were a conservative reaction to the red scare and included loyalty oaths which teachers in that state were required to take as proof of their patriotism and opposition to communism. Dewey's opposition to the Lusk laws was adamant ("we are still hunting heretics among our school teachers"); communism is an hypothesis which, like any other, is fair game for classroom inquiry at some (relatively advanced) stage of the learning process and may not be ruled out by educational authorities on grounds of patriotism or anything else.[33] Since we do not know whether the theory is false until we investigate it, the proper course is to present the facts as we know them and allow the students to reason it out in the usual way. Even when a preponderance of political theorists or democratic voters has examined and rejected the idea, for educational purposes it remains unknown in advance of inquiry whether it can withstand criticism or not. But for what is clearly incontrovertible, in principle, it is unknowable what an educated mind will choose to believe, and teachers who wish for any reason to control this are stepping out of their role as educators and into the role of activists and propagandists. Still more important for Dewey than the freedom to think and speak is the freedom to work or to pursue an investigation wherever it leads and to let the proverbial chips fall where they may. This kind of freedom pertains not only to what can be outwardly expressed in a given institution but, more importantly perhaps, to its general environment or ethos: "It is an intangible, undefinable affair; something which is in the atmosphere and operates as a continuous and unconscious stimulus. It affects the spirit in which the university as a whole does its work, rather than the overt expressions of any one individual."[34] The freedom to form one's own educational ends, to pursue one's interests, form judgments, and so on, is neither unlimited nor an end in itself but is an imperative in the extent to which it is conducive to rational inquiry. This is not a philosophy of do what you feel but do the work that needs to be done as it needs to be done. It is the "freedom of intelligence" that he was speaking of, and it is a point that friendly and unfriendly readers alike have routinely misunderstood.[35]

This brings us to the vexed question of progressive education. For a century, Dewey's name has been associated with this movement, although to speak of him as one of its apologists, as many continue to do, is approximately half correct. Its principal American representatives at this time were Francis W. Parker and William Heard Kilpatrick, and while Dewey's name has long been included in this group he expressed numerous and profound reservations about a movement in educational thinking that was claiming him as an influence while showing not more than a tangential relation to his philosophy. One might say that Dewey was to progressive education what Marx was to the Soviet Union—an inspiration, an influence, and an often-cited name but not exactly a proponent. Unlike Marx, Dewey did live to see the movement that claimed him as one of their own carry their (and some of his) ideas into practice in ways that were transforming much of American schooling in fundamental ways, and while Dewey and the progressives were largely on the same page with respect to their criticisms of traditional education, they differed significantly on what was to replace it. All theorists and practitioners connected with this movement were calling for an end to rote learning, whole-class instruction, discipline and effort over freedom and interest, teacher-centered classrooms, a standardized curriculum, and an ethos of aristocracy and authoritarianism. On the question of what model was to replace this, however, differences abounded, and much of what the general movement was practicing would be criticized directly by Dewey, most especially in his important text of 1938, *Experience and Education.*

Among his major criticisms in that book is the charge that a great deal of progressive education amounted merely to a pendulum swing from one extreme to the other, resulting in a system that was no better than what it replaced. Never given to extremes or grand oppositions, Dewey rejected the false choice that progressives and traditionalists were proffering: "development from within" versus "formation from without"; freedom versus order; child-centered versus teacher- or curriculum-centered; intellectual capacity versus information and memory work; internal versus external direction; present activity versus preparation for the future, and so on. As he remarked, "in spite of itself any movement that thinks and acts in terms of an 'ism becomes so involved in reaction against other 'isms that it is unwittingly controlled by them."[36] A philosophy of anti-_______ism is likely to reproduce in a new form whatever fills in the blank, whether we are speaking of education, politics, or anything else, for it is forever taking unwitting direction from the position it is rejecting and offering up a course overcorrection that still lands us in a ditch. Progressivism was a reactionary scheme which, in Dewey's estimation, succeeded little or perhaps no better than what it sought to replace. Its specific shortcomings are several: it throws out the baby of conventional education (an organized curriculum, acquiring information, reading books) with the bathwater; it misconstrues his appeal to students' interests as a call to dumb down the whole business of education; it mistakes free inquiry for aimless activity; it modifies his accent on the teacher as a leader of group activities into a view of the teacher as a bystander; it effects a simple pendulum swing from teacher- to student-centered education; it replaces regimentation with pandemonium, and some others.

Both advocates and critics of progressive education have long mistaken Dewey as a champion of a student-centered approach despite his clearly stated opposition to this. His Copernican revolution was intended to shift the center of gravity from the teacher toward not the students themselves but the students' experience and more specifically the relation between the students' experience and the subject matter. We are back to Dewey's notion of interaction: it is not the child him- or herself who stands in the center but their intelligent interaction with a curriculum that fosters growth, although he would at times offer statements which read without context appeared to support the child-centered view. Student-centeredness was a mere reversal of teacher-centeredness, and here again was a simple duality which this profoundly dialectical thinker rejected for a view in which teacher, students, students' experience, and subject matter are dynamically interrelated in the practice of inquiry. The intellectual growth of the student is the intended outcome, but this does not entail that the student stands in the center. Inquiry—an activity in which students, the teacher, and some object of knowledge are mutually bound up—is the heart of education, and his rejection of the conventional model for ignoring the students' interests and experience was matched with a rejection of the progressive alternative for ignoring the subject matter and demoting the teacher to an onlooker. The kind of growth of which he was speaking does not occur by leaving students to do as they will:

> Now such a method is really stupid. For it attempts the impossible, which is always stupid; and it misconceives the conditions of independent thinking. There are a multitude of ways of reacting

to surrounding conditions, and without some guidance from experience these reactions are almost sure to be casual, sporadic and ultimately fatiguing, accompanied by nervous strain. Since the teacher has presumably a greater background of experience, there is the same presumption of the right of a teacher to make suggestions as to what to do, as there is on the part of the head carpenter to suggest to apprentices something of what they are to do.[37]

Between the student and the curriculum there is no opposition but a vital interaction in which the teacher is also a participant, not to be sure in the manner of an autocrat but as a leader and a guide.

As with each of the preceding chapters, there are many further details that warrant examination which I shall not go into here. The larger picture of Dewey's social philosophy is of a democratic way of life in which an educated citizenry continually inquires on a cooperative and rational basis into the problems of their time and searches for pragmatic resolutions to the difficulties that every social order faces. It is no utopian vision of "public deliberation" in a rationalistic sense of the phrase but a conception in which citizens are intelligent participants in the contested affairs of social life while their educational institutions foster the kind of growth that makes such participation possible.

Notes

1 Dewey, *A Common Faith*, MW 9 (1934), 22.

2 Dewey, *The School and Society*, MW 1 (1900), 10.

3 Dewey, "The Need for a Philosophy of Education," LW 9 (1934), 194.

4 Dewey, *Democracy and Education*, MW 9 (1916), 107.

5 Dewey, *Experience and Education*, LW 13 (1938), 62.

6 Dewey, "The Sources of a Science of Education," LW 5 (1929), 9.

7 Dewey, "A Pedagogical Experiment," EW 5 (1896), 245.

8 Dewey, "Progressive Education and the Science of Education," LW 3 (1928), 258.

9 Dewey, *The School and Society*, MW 1 (1900), 24.

10 Dewey, "How the Mind Learns," LW 17 (1901), 214.

11 Dewey, *Experience and Education*, LW 13 (1938), 37.

12 Dewey, *Democracy and Education*, MW 9 (1916), 30, 165.

13 Dewey, *The Child and the Curriculum*, MW 2 (1903), 277–8.

14 Dewey, *Experience and Education*, LW 13 (1938), 11.

15 Dewey, "Education, Direct and Indirect," MW 3 (1909), 240.

16 Dewey, *Democracy and Education*, MW 9 (1916), 82.

17 Dewey, "Interest in Relation to Training of the Will," EW 5 (1896), 142.

18 This continues to the present day. Only yesterday did I read a newspaper editorial that castigated Dewey at length for the many failures of contemporary education, written by someone claiming a knowledge of Dewey's thought that is evidently not informed by reading his work. A quick skim of *Democracy and Education* would have disabused the writer of his obvious misinterpretations, and the same can be said of countless books on education that have appeared over the decades and which I shall not cite here.

19 Dewey, *Democracy and Education*, MW 9 (1916), 59.

20 Dewey, *Experience and Education*, LW 13 (1938), 21.

21 Dewey, *Experience and Education*, LW 13 (1938), 24, 26. The phrase "objective conditions" that Dewey employs here "includes what is done by the educator and the way in which it is done, not only words spoken but the tone of voice in which they are spoken. It includes equipment, books, apparatus, toys, games played. It includes the materials with which an individual interacts, and, most important of all, the total *social* set-up of the conditions in which a person is engaged." Dewey, *Experience and Education*, LW 13 (1938), 26.

22 Dewey, "The Evolutionary Method As Applied to Morality," MW 1 (1902), 11.

23 Dewey, *Democracy and Education*, MW 9 (1916), 91, 44.

24 Dewey, *How We Think*, LW 8 (1933), 160.

25 Dewey, "The Challenge of Democracy to Education," LW 11 (1937), 185.

26 Dewey, "Academic Freedom," MW 2 (1902), 64.

27 Dewey, "The Liberal College and its Enemies," MW 15 (1924), 208; Dewey, *Democracy and Education*, MW 9 (1916), 71.

28 Dewey, *How We Think*, LW 8 (1933), 347.

29 Dewey, *Democracy and Education*, MW 9 (1916), 50.

30 Dewey, "Teaching That Does Not Educate," MW 4 (1909), 202.

31 Dewey, *How We Think*, LW 8 (1933), 147–8.

32 Dewey, "Freedom in Workers' Education," LW 5 (1929), 332.

33 Dewey, "Report of Interview with John Dewey," with Charles W. Wood, MW 13 (1922), 430.

34 Dewey, "Academic Freedom," MW 2 (1902), 61.

35 Dewey, *Experience and Education*, LW 13 (1938), 39.

36 Dewey, *Experience and Education*, LW 13 (1938), 5.

37 Dewey, "Individuality and Experience," LW 2 (1926), 59.

7

Philosophy of Religion

Dewey remains best known for his contributions to the theory of knowledge, politics, and education, although the thirty-eight volumes of his complete works include major writings on nearly every major subdiscipline of the philosophy of his time, including two which the present and following chapter will examine. Prior to the 1930s one finds few major statements from Dewey on either aesthetics or the philosophy of religion, which is not a testament to a lack of interest in or opinions about either subject, but it would not be until a relatively late stage in his career that his mature reflections on both topics would appear. *Art as Experience* (1934) would represent a culmination of a lifetime of reflection on the aesthetic and will be the topic of Chapter 8, while *A Common Faith* (also 1934) accomplished much the same in the philosophy of religion. Both were unusual works which fit somewhat awkwardly into the literature of their time, and the former perhaps somewhat more so than the latter. *A Common Faith* will be our focus in this chapter with some reference to other works but much less so than previous chapters have done for reason of the relative paucity of remarks that we find in his writings prior to this relatively brief text.

Dewey never lacked interest in religion, although one might have thought so prior to 1932 when he delivered the series of lectures at Yale University upon which this book was based. Raised a devout

Protestant, he remained a member of the Congregational Church until the age of thirty-five, which coincided with his move in 1894 from the University of Michigan to the University of Chicago. His reasons for leaving that church are elusive; his growing attraction toward naturalism and pragmatism may have created a tension in his mind with the Hegelian-Christian synthesis of his early period, but a better explanation may be that the sort of real-world problems that concerned him were in his view better resolved within the secular mode of thought he was developing than in more traditional religious frameworks. He was never the strident atheist that a Feuerbach or a Marx had been; it would be better to say that religion did not significantly factor into his philosophical project until the Yale lectures afforded an occasion to reflect on what if any place the religious could hold in the philosophy he was defending and in modern culture more broadly. His aim, as one scholar points out, is to engage in a similar exercise in "reconstruction" in the area of religion as what he had been attempting in so many other areas of thought, "to find the vital core of the historically religious life and to nurture this core in ways appropriate to our lives."[1] The great world religions, Dewey maintained, provided various articulations or manifestations of an underlying "vital core" which is separable from the belief systems themselves and capable of receiving a secular interpretation which better suits modern conditions. In formulating this argument, he took his place in a movement of sorts whose watchwords include demythologization and secularization. He was of the view that traditional religion's fundamental—especially its more worldly—aims are better pursued in the kind of social philosophy that he had been developing, while ritual, tradition, sacred texts, the priesthood, and so on were extraneous to its true purpose. His reconstruction of religion was to be naturalistic and stand against all supernaturalism. At its heart would be a distinction between "religion" and "the religious," about which we shall have more to say in due course, but its central point is to separate the wheat from the chaff while bringing "the religious" into coherence with the content and spirit of modern science. Dewey was not an unspiritual person, but he had little regard for organized religion and the dogmatism that he associated with it. The conception of "the religious" that he would articulate would be more attitudinal than doctrinal, worldly rather than otherworldly, secular rather than sacred, and it would have nothing to do with churches. After leaving the Congregationalists he would never return to an organized faith community but preferred to speak of "natural piety" and the "religious aspect of experience" in a way that owed relatively little to tradition.

Dewey's reflections on the religious proceed from the observation that the Western world had been witnessing a decline in religious observance and belief and an associated decline of trust in many of the traditional authorities that include but are not limited to organized religion. This historical and sociological fact is a matter of the highest importance and provides an occasion to pose the question of spirituality anew. The significance of the historical trend, as he saw it, is not restricted to the relative decline in church membership and attendance but extends to religion's

decline as a vitally integrative and directive force in men's thought and sentiments. Whether even in the ages of the past that are called religious, religion was itself the actively central force that it is sometimes said to have been may be doubted. But it cannot be doubted that it was the symbol of the existence of conditions and forces that gave unity and a centre to men's views of life. It at least gathered together in weighty and shared symbols a sense of the objects to which men were so attached as to have support and stay in their outlook on life.[2]

In a secular society, religiosity is no longer part of the common and taken-for-granted intellectual heritage but a matter that is decidedly optional and which is increasingly opted against, most often on grounds of its ostensible conflict with science. This optional character of religion, he noted, is a fact of profound importance for it brings about a deep realignment not only in our shared worldview but in the way of life that is bound up with it, with conceptions of morality and culture which for untold centuries were the glue that held societies together. The modern "transfer of interest from the eternal and universal to what is changing and specific, concrete," together with "the general decay of the authority of fixed institutions and class distinctions and relations" has effected a recentering of modern life toward scientific and democratic problem-solving in a way that Dewey saw as largely commendable.[3] Secularization entails that not only the state but social institutions and practices in general no longer revolve around a church and that the latter instead "is a *special* institution within a secular community."[4] It is a logical extension of the transition from Roman Catholic to Protestant Christianity which saw a renewed accent upon the relation of the individual conscience and its creator along with a partial jettisoning of received theological beliefs. Whatever progress had occurred in modern times, on his view, was accomplished in the main independently of ecclesiastic organizations, and it might be anticipated that future improvements in the general realm of worldly affairs would owe more to the application of experimental inquiry than to belief systems of old.

Philosophy itself may be understood as having emerged historically from religion and as bearing a mission that vitally concerns the latter, which is "to extract the essential moral kernel out of the threatened traditional beliefs of the past. . . . It became the work of philosophy to justify on rational grounds the spirit, though not the form, of accepted beliefs and traditional customs."[5] If much of the grist to philosophy's mill from its origins to the present time consists in such customary beliefs, its business remains one of critiquing and refining this material while turning it to a pragmatic purpose. Part of philosophy's inheritance from religion is a sense of the uncertainty and insecurity that lie at the heart of the human condition. The natural and human world is an unstable mix of fortunate and threatening circumstances, in which change is ubiquitous and human action is a precarious but at times intelligent gamble: "The world is a scene of risk; it is uncertain, unstable, uncannily unstable. Its dangers are irregular, inconstant, not to be counted upon as to their times and seasons. . . . Plague, famine, failure of crops, disease, death, defeat in battle, are always just around the corner, and so are abundance, strength, victory, festival and song."[6] Traditional religion as Dewey saw it constituted a means of coping with such a world but in a manner that reflected the time period and the culture in which it arose. A scientific age demands a turn toward the secular, and in matters that concern not only the natural sciences but human life broadly conceived. If the latter has for millennia been the preserve of religion, what is now called for in the "ever-recurring struggle between darkness and knowledge" is that a knowledge that bears upon life be liberated from "a rearguard of ignorance, prejudice, dogma, routine, tradition."[7]

The latter sentiment combined with his decades-long silence on the subject might incline us to expect Dewey to part ways with religion in its entirety, until seemingly from out of nowhere came *A Common Faith*. The central argument of this book turns upon a distinction he would draw between "religion" and "the religious," and it is to this question that we now turn. By religion Dewey intended a system of myths, rituals, values, practices, customs, a priesthood, and an institution that are all organized around a common set of beliefs, many of which concern the supernatural and the otherworldly. His opposition to religion in this sense of the term stems from the beliefs themselves or the intellectual content that holds the membership of a given theological movement together. Without attempting a thoroughgoing refutation of particular belief systems, his argument draws attention to the organic connection between a historical religion and the culture in which it arose and asks "how much in religions now accepted are survivals from outgrown cultures." Cultures come and go, but it is a common occurrence for beliefs that enabled a given historical community to cope with their experience to persist long after the culture is modified or left behind, in which case the ideas in question are not refuted so much as outdated. Under this condition a belief in the supernatural is especially suspect, and Dewey saw no role for this in the modern world. Religion on his definition is inseparable from an intellectual commitment to the supernatural, and it is a commitment that a scientific naturalism has superseded. The supernatural refers to "unseen powers" of one kind or another, from

> the vague and undefined Mana of the Melanesians [to] the Kami of primitive Shintoism; the fetish of the Africans; spirits, having some human properties, that pervade natural places and animate natural forces; the ultimate and impersonal principle of Buddhism; the unmoved mover of Greek thought; the gods and semi-divine heroes of the Greek and Roman Pantheons; the personal and loving Providence of Christianity, omnipotent, and limited by a corresponding evil power; the arbitrary Will of Moslemism; the supreme legislator and judge of deism.[8]

Dewey saw little worth salvaging in any of the above, although as we shall see he did preserve a somewhat idiosyncratic conception of God.

What he was concerned to reject is "the intellectual side of the religious attitude," or the theological dimension rather than the dispositional.[9] A scientific order has no place for religion in this sense, and where we must speak of particular religions rather than religion simpliciter. The latter connotes nothing at all; a religion is a distinct system of beliefs concerning "unseen powers," and no common denominator underlies all such systems. The "moral kernel" he would attempt to extract need presuppose nothing regarding the supernatural and indeed is best served by divesting it of whatever cultural-historical vestiges remain when these run afoul of modern science. The kernel itself is neutral with respect to the supernatural and the dogmatic, with Dewey opting here as in every other area of his philosophy for naturalism and inquiry. His charge against the major world religions—his focus, as one might expect, was primarily upon the Abrahamic faiths—of intellectual bankruptcy bears in significant part upon the notion of special, revealed truths. No knowledge or truth of any kind, he would always insist, is to be had apart from experimental inquiry, and sacred texts do not inquire but proclaim. The content of what they announce stands or falls on the method by which this is ostensibly known, and revelation is not a method.

Anyone hoping to find in this short book (or anywhere else in his writings) a detailed analysis of particular theological systems will be disappointed as its author was content to express a broad-ranging critique of historical religions generally. The extent of his knowledge of religions other than that of his youth does appear to have been limited; the references in the index volume of his complete works to Roman Catholicism, for instance, are relatively few and exhibit not more than a superficial familiarity, while the same can be said of various other non-Protestant faiths. What, then, was he rejecting and for what reasons? The short answer is anything and everything that falls under the umbrella of revelation, and in particular any beliefs that are not hypotheses testable by the same methodology as is applicable across the board of human knowledge. What many a theological doctrine amounts to, in his view, is an emotionally overcharged projection onto the world (or a world beyond this world) of a set of ideals which may be entirely legitimate when regarded as ideals alone without the theological baggage. As he expressed it, "The inherent vice of all intellectual schemes of idealism," both religious and metaphysical, "is that they convert the idealism of action into a system of beliefs about antecedent reality." Further, "these schemes inevitably glide into alliance with the supernatural," when they would have been better served by remaining on a level of moral ideals.[10] The critique of religion, then, is at once moral, epistemological, and psychological: the religious believer commits the intellectual and psychological error of projecting their ideals onto an otherworldly plane without an epistemological basis and while weakening the ideals themselves by overloading them with a baggage they cannot bear. In place of arguments they substitute the sheer insistence that a sacred text or organization possesses a cache of truths not otherwise accessible to the individual. The appeal to the supernatural ends up blocking the road of inquiry into how the very ideals a religion prizes might be effectively realized.

Whatever truths are to be had in religious worldviews amount to values or ideals which are ill-served by their theological trappings. As he categorically stated, "The opposition between religious values as I conceive them and religions is not to be bridged. Just because the release of these values is so important, their identification with the creeds and cults of religions must be dissolved." Values of justice, truth, beauty, happiness, or freedom are best pursued through cooperative intelligence and without the metaphysical and mythical ornamentations that religions have imposed upon them. It is little improvement, he added, when liberal theologians translate religious ideas of old into symbols, for "Of what are the beliefs symbols?" What does a belief in the soul or the holy trinity symbolize—a transcendent reality or an object of ordinary experience? The notion of special experiences revealing truths not available to experience in its more mundane forms invites skepticism, Dewey believed, and if such values are available to ordinary experience then would they not be properly pursued directly rather than through the mediation of culturally outmoded symbols? If what we are speaking of is beliefs, symbolism can only be an obstacle to the manner of thinking that beliefs in general call for. Inquiry is all there is; he allows no separation of faith and knowledge or revealed and prosaic truth. Faith itself is neither evidentiary nor a special form of knowledge but, as he cited John Locke, "assent to a proposition . . . on the credit of its proposer."[11] Faith, for Dewey, is cognitive and propositional, and anything fitting this description remains subject to the same investigative procedures as all other areas of belief. An appeal to revealed dogma can only be a crutch employed by those who are determined to believe without evidence something that is psychologically satisfying.

"There is," he categorically stated in the same text, "but one sure road of access to truth—the road of patient, cooperative inquiry operating by means of observation, experiment, record and controlled reflection."[12] So far this looks like textbook religious skepticism with the customary accent on empiricism, but Dewey did not rest his case on this point. There is more to "the religious" than "religion," where again by the latter he meant a set of propositional statements regarding the supernatural and otherworldly. The religious attitude bears at once upon beliefs, which are unworthy of assent if they do not result from inquiry in his sense of the term, and ideals or values which are often worth conserving provided they can be liberated from their erstwhile cultural and theological trappings. Here matters become somewhat more complex, as is evident from the curiously infrequent remarks in his educational writings on the subject of religious education. A thoroughgoing atheist might be expected to maintain that all religious instruction is miseducative, but Dewey declined to take this view, instead asserting that "the most fundamental of all educational questions [are] the moral and religious." What could this mean? It is clearly not that educators are to see to it that students adopt a given set of theological beliefs, but what is his positive meaning? The answer appears to be that while teachers must refrain from instilling any controversial viewpoint in students' minds, the reasons they must do so include not only that this amounts to an indoctrination which is the antithesis of true education but the additional consideration that "to force prematurely upon the child either the mature ideas or the spiritual emotions of the adult is to run the risk of a fundamental danger, that of forestalling future deeper experiences which might otherwise in their season become personal realities to him."[13] It is on grounds not of their falsity but of their importance in later life that such matters are rightly excluded from the classroom, as one might exclude other mature subject matters from minds too young to digest them. We see Dewey here recognizing the profound importance of that with which religion concerns itself, but in what, in his estimation, does its value consist? What are "the mature ideas or the spiritual emotions of the adult" to which he was alluding? Not beliefs apparently, or not beliefs of a theological nature, but instead what he termed "the religious quality of experience" which is more attitudinal than doctrinal. "I am not proposing a religion," as he put it,

> but rather the emancipation of elements and outlooks that may be called religious. For the moment we have a religion, whether that of the Sioux Indian or of Judaism or of Christianity, that moment the ideal factors in experience that may be called religious take on a load that is not inherent in them, a load of current beliefs and of institutional practices that are irrelevant to them.[14]

What is clear in his view is that the "quality of experience" to which he was referring is devitalized by belief, and so much so that anything that meets his definition of a religion actively prevents such experience from appearing owing to the dogmatic and cultural baggage that accompanies it. Jettison the baggage and religious experience becomes possible. More elusive is what has now become possible?

Is religious experience qualitatively distinct from experience in its other, more everyday, forms, from moral experience to social, political, aesthetic, empirical, educational, and so on? A negative answer is suggested right away by Dewey's habit of viewing the various dimensions of human experience in their organic interconnectedness rather than as wholly discrete or from the dynamic of the organism negotiating its way through a world. He would speak in the text upon which we have been dwelling of "the religious phase of experience" and "the religious aspect of experience" rather than "religious experience" itself, as if the latter were a separate compartment accessed by separate means and revealing separate truths. It neither stands aloof from experience in its more mundane varieties nor, as many were arguing, affords a foundation for a given religion. There is not "a definite kind of experience which is itself religious"; rather, "'religious' as a quality of experience signifies something that may belong to all these [moral, empirical, aesthetic, etc.] experiences. It is the polar opposite of some type of experience that can exist by itself." We have no need of sanctuaries or sacred spaces in Dewey's decidedly worldly way of thinking but the veritable antithesis: a turn of mind that is strongly attuned to ideals of this world but in their deeper and more personal dimension. One can have a religious experience of justice, for example, through commitment to a social cause that strikes a deeper note within the self than the merely strategic or contingent, a comportment that is more like devotion. An artist may adopt a religious attitude toward the products of one's creation or regard such works as mere objects of pleasure, entertainment, or profit. One can, it appears, be religious in this sense about anything that has a depth dimension to it and whose meaning is capable of resonating within our experience on a more profound register than the everyday. The religious quality in an experience pertains to nothing inherent in its object but to "its function" and to "the *effect* produced" within the subject or, better, between subject and object. It is a quality that crucially bears upon "the better adjustment in life and its conditions." What function, effect, or manner of adjustment is this? There is a roughly Kierkegaardian "taking to heart" that is at work here, but it is not a subjective process alone but a reciprocal modification of conditions both within and without the self, an adaptation that is no mere submission but an active transformation of conditions in the world, something intermediate between action and passion. In becoming devoted to a cause or an ideal, one is effecting a change in these conditions while, as he put it, "there are also changes in ourselves in relation to the world in which we live that are much more inclusive and deep seated. They relate not to this and that want in relation to this and that condition of our surroundings, but pertain to our being in its entirety. Because of their scope, this modification of ourselves is enduring."[15] One is transformed in the same process by which one transforms or acts in the world in the pursuit of an ideal of one kind or another.

At the root of the religious attitude, then, is a pursuit of worldly ideals that is simultaneously self- and world-transforming. The "adjustment" it achieves between the person and their world is not a one-way adaptation; rather, the "note of submission" that it includes is both freely undergone and more active than "a mere Stoical resolution to endure unperturbed throughout the buffetings of fortune." If this attitude is historically accompanied by a theology, the latter for Dewey is an extraneous accompaniment which more often hampers the pursuit of the ends that it valorizes. This factor, in his view, goes some way toward explaining the decline of religious participation that the modern West is witnessing. The "weight of historic encumbrances" not limited to beliefs in the supernatural poses a formidable obstacle to the kind of experiences we are speaking of as religious. Certain moral beliefs along with some of the realities associated with ecclesiastic institutions further contribute toward the deterioration of what such organizations set out to promote. It is a frequent occurrence, he noted, for some to be so put off by the institutional forms of religion that they end up abandoning both religions and the attitudes and ideals that might have been cultivated in the more secular manner that Dewey preferred. Spiritual and moral impoverishment is a frequent consequence of this throwing out of the baby with the bathwater, and this phenomenon goes some way toward explaining the sense of malaise that he believed to be on the rise in modern times. Religion is an encumbrance to the religious, both in causing many to jettison values they ought to be pursuing and in blocking the path by which they are optimally pursued. The Hegelian in Dewey was always alive to tradition and to the imperative of conserving whatever elements of it are worth not only transmitting to the young but "reconstructing" when they become moribund, and it is precisely on this note that he ends this book:

We who now live are parts of a humanity that extends into the remote past, a humanity that has interacted with nature. The things in civilization we most prize are not of ourselves. They exist by grace of the doings and sufferings of the continuous human community in which we are a link. Ours is the responsibility of conserving, transmitting, rectifying, and expanding the heritage of values we have received that those who come after us may receive it more solid and secure, more widely accessible and more generously shared than we have received it. Here are all the elements for a religious faith that shall not be confined to sect, class, or race. Such a faith has always been implicitly the common faith of mankind. It remains to make it explicit and militant.[16]

These are not the words of an atheist but of a moralist with a sensibility that is in a sense both liberal and conservative in his aspiration to revivify ideals largely of old by adapting them to the conditions of modern life. We see him here as in other areas of his thought resisting dichotomies of objectivism and subjectivism, absolutism and relativism, and so on. Religious experience, as he spoke of it, for instance, is not radically subjective, as the accent on experience so often implies, for it bears upon ideals that are socially shared, which belong to a cultural heritage, and which are pursued not only in the privacy of our inwardness but still more in our public lives. The conviction and loyalty they inspire do produce a certain resonance and unification within the subject, but religious experience is not an exercise in self-indulgence or empty emotionalism for it is fundamentally outward-looking in its orientation toward realizing social ends by natural means. A thoroughgoing subjectivism is ruled out, as is an objectivism or absolutism that renders the ideals of which we have been speaking as any kind of metaphysical beings that are above the order of nature. The theological imagination that hypostasizes and projects onto a higher realm the kind of values that the religious attitude is properly concerned with may be put aside in favor of an outlook that is wholly of this world.

Where does this leave mystical experience? Is there any room in Dewey's conception of the religious for the mystical or a mysticism of some kind, given the strong accent in all his work upon experience in its various dimensions? William James' *Varieties of Religious Experience* of 1902 had investigated various experiences that he regarded as mystical, yet Dewey would not follow suit in this, instead remarking only briefly on a phenomenon that appears to have held little interest for him. What is philosophically interesting in such experiences, he noted, is whether they are revelatory in a sense of affording a basis for beliefs that is not available otherwise, and here his answer is negative. He did not deny that experiences called mystical by many of those who have them exist. Indeed, they do; the existence of such experiences is a "fact." But the philosophically important matter is the "interpretation of the fact." This fact, like any other, calls for inquiry, and the belief that this experience provides its experiencer with access to a set of truths is properly regarded as a hypothesis which, although it may not be ruled out *a priori*, does need to be tested in the usual way. To declare that mystical experience is specially revelatory and that we know this by means of the same kind of experience is question-begging. The main point of his brief remarks on this question is not to proffer a hypothesis regarding mystical experience but to deny the epistemic separation between this and more ordinary forms of experience. He rejected both a metaphysical dualism of natural and supernatural and an epistemological dualism of experimental inquiry into matters of this world and mystical experience into what lies beyond or any notion of the latter as having special authority in a particular region of knowledge. The closest to an hypothesis Dewey would come on this issue is to speculate that mystical experiences may be less special and more common than we think, that "in some degree of intensity, they occur so frequently that they may be regarded as normal manifestations that take place at certain rhythmic points in the movement of experience."[17] The idea of rhythmic points in our experience is one to which we shall return in the following chapter, but for now Dewey was content to remark briefly on mystical experience in a largely skeptical vein. In the background lay his more general skepticism regarding an idealism or romanticism that professes a "supreme regard for the inner meaning of things, reverence for inner truth in disregard of external consequences of advantage or disadvantage, [which he held to be] . . . the distinguishing mark of the German spirit."[18] Dewey was not above a nationalism that at times went beyond the political to the cultural and philosophical, most clearly evidenced by the book just cited from 1915.

His conception of "the religious" would never receive the kind of clarity for which Dewey typically strove in his work, which may be explainable in part by his own reported experiences of the mystical. His experience with organized religion did not inspire a lifelong commitment, as we have seen, nor does it seem to have motivated him to undertake serious research into any of the great world religions other than that of his youth. Dewey's experience of the religious and the mystical includes an important episode when he was twenty years old during which he later reported experiencing a profound oneness with the world reminiscent of the poetic descriptions of Whitman and Wordsworth, an experience of a felt harmony both with the universe in its totality and within himself. He would offer no detailed account or theoretical explanation of this experience, but it bore a personal significance that remained with him through life. Our ever-sober philosopher would neither wax poetic on the subject nor speculate in his writings as to the nature or cause of his experience, our knowledge of this episode coming only from a report to a friend he would relate years after the fact. The experience does not appear to have been dramatic but instead a perception of deep well-being, trust, and quiet contentment. He may well have had this episode in mind when in *A Common Faith* he spoke of a "deep-seated harmonizing of the self with the Universe (as a name for the totality of conditions with which the self is connected)." As usual, he offered no philosophical explanation of such an experience, noting only that subconscious factors may play as large a role in this kind of perception as anything metaphysical, and that "this composing of the self" happens "only through imagination."[19] The religious attitude, it seems, is not for the unimaginative, although he was far from dismissing it as a merely psychological phenomenon. His reluctance to hazard an hypothesis suggests that a philosophical undecideability may be at work here, in the face of which it is preferable to cultivate humility than any definite belief. Human existence is bound up with forces beyond our command and our knowledge, and we may be alive to this without rushing in with theological explanations.

Whether this is properly describable as agnosticism, pantheism, atheism, or some other classification is about equally doubtful, and Dewey himself refrained from designating his position with any such label. His stance on Christianity would remain decidedly ambiguous with remarkably few biblical references appearing in this text and throughout his writings. The idea of God itself does make an appearance, however. He proposes that the word properly connotes either what he calls "a particular Being" of one kind or another or "the unity of all ideal ends arousing us to desire and actions," and opts decidedly for the latter. If we can continue to speak of God at all, he maintained, it is not as a substance or any kind of metaphysical existent but as a moral phenomenon that is inseparable from the kind of ideals alluded to above. The distinction between religion and the religious turns in large part upon a notion of God as a supernatural being or as an experiential "unification of ideal values that is essentially imaginative in origin when the imagination supervenes in conduct," and where the imaginative is not regarded in simple opposition to the real. He wanted no part of a God that is a metaphysical being, but the idea of God and the word itself ought to be retained as a name for the "uniting of the ideal and actual." Dewey's penchant for unifying the disparate or regarding in organic connectedness what often appears as categorially opposed is visible here again, as at the heart of the religious attitude is a vision of the human being not in isolation or that stands to its fellows as Hobbesian atoms in a materialist universe but as a participant in a world that also sustains us. What is sustaining is the project of harmonizing values—he mentions as examples art, knowledge, effort, rest, education, fellowship, friendship, love, mental and physical growth—which are not individual creations but exist in the world in "relatively embryonic" form with our actions, of bringing ideals that are largely received and inchoate to bear upon conditions of real life, and in ways that inspire a commitment that is neither passionless nor fleeting.[20] Why this ought to be designated as "God" is elusive, but he was not content to abandon the word but sought to retain it while refashioning it to suit a scientific and democratic worldview.[21] The term agnosticism he disavowed as a half-hearted rejection of both the supernatural and the God of metaphysics. It is generally wise to acknowledge our intellectual finitude, but the agnostic's error is to opt out of a debate in which it is urgent that we take a stand. We are to affirm the supernatural or foreswear it, and Dewey's commitment to naturalism inclined him toward the latter. The "common faith of mankind" is a moral, not metaphysical, faith in ideals which are realizable in this world, which are capable of reconciling the individual both with himself or herself and with their fellow citizens, and which must not be the preserve of a subsection of the population.[22] The responsibility of one and all is to transmit such values to the next generation while working to broaden their availability and application in the conditions in which we find ourselves.

Many a theist would take issue with Dewey's use of the word God, of course, for its connection with the entire history of the concept is rather tenuous. Another term might have captured his meaning, and his reasons for employing this word rather than another are not especially strong. One such reason is his repudiation of the kind of atheism that was on the march during his lifetime in both the academic world and the broader culture. By his time it had become usual for an intellectual and social reformer to disavow religion and faith in all their forms, and Dewey followed suit only to a point. He was on board with metaphysical-theological skepticism, but where he differed from a Marx or a Mill was on the issue of what he spoke of as a "natural piety" which he sensed was lacking in the general movement toward atheism. This is not the piety of the believer but a somewhat more poetic attitude or sensibility. It contains a note of submission but is not acquiescent; instead it is humble, non-narcissistic, and non-alienated. It is no idealization or naive acceptance of the way things are, but nor does it fly to the opposite extreme of a militant desire to smash the system or recreate the world in the image of oneself. It is "pious" in its quiet humility and it is "natural" in its sense of nature as that in which we are all participants and as a totality in which the individual is not more than a part but a part that is also purposive and rational. What he called "aggressive atheism" stands in opposition to "traditional supernaturalism" only outwardly; inwardly, both are concerned with the human being as an alienated atom and the measure of all things, nature being relegated to an inferior position relative to the apex that is the individual: "A religious attitude . . . needs the sense of a connection of man, in the way of both dependence and support, with the enveloping world that the imagination feels is a universe. Use of the words 'God' or 'divine' to convey the union of actual with ideal may protect man from a sense of isolation and from consequent despair or defiance." Atheism is the stance of the defiant teenager and notional center of existence, its militancy symptomatic of an anomie which ends in cynicism: "The attitude taken is often that of man living in an indifferent and hostile world and issuing blasts of defiance," where what is preferable is a perspective on existence that is less rancorous and more deeply bound up with one's social and natural environment.[23]

A final point concerns experiences of transcendence and meaning. We do not encounter meaning, he maintained, solely in the realm of the material and "pragmatic" in a narrow connotation of the word. A starry-eyed dreamer Dewey was not, but he was equally far removed from an arid rationalism in speaking of the world of human experience as saturated with meanings which are abundant, multifarious, and more than occasionally enigmatic. There are experiences of meaning—many of them—that transcend the mundane and which resist efforts at easy classification. As Victor Kestenbaum has pointed out,

> Dewey's "road of meaning" moves from the finite to the infinite, from the visible to the invisible, from the material to the spiritual, from the concrete to the transcendent—and then back. Dewey is not just an empiricist; he is an *excellent* empiricist. He understands that transcendentally distant places sometimes offer the promise of "a more than common meaning."[24]

"Excellent empiricist" is an apt description and so is phenomenologist; phenomenologically, our experience is organic, rhythmic, interconnected, purposive, and variously tangible and intangible, habitual and surprising, and structured and anomalous. It is not reducible to atomic elements such as sense data or raw percepts upon which the mind later goes to work but is always already meaningful and on the way in one fashion or another. The religious attitude is especially attuned toward the intangible and transcendent, to that which lies beyond the reach of secure knowledge but that demands our attention for reasons of its evident import and intimations of meanings and ideals that may be transformative. We may either be alive to the transcendent or closed to it, and Dewey's preference for the former is not a rational holiday but a consequence of an intellectual stance that is in every case experimental and undogmatic. The experimental mind is not so risk-averse as to stop in its tracks in every instance of uncertainty. Indeed, it is in the nature of experiential growth to press onward in a way that is exploratory and tentative while also unafraid and at times bold. The "road of meaning" to which Kestenbaum alludes is reciprocal, moving out into the speculative and back again, constantly testing its suppositions while also prepared to be surprised at what it encounters. Transcendent ideals are inchoate and intangible, but they need be neither absolute nor wholly mystical. It is the bringing into union of all such ideals, from the relatively known to the elusive and emerging, with the conditions of real life that the religious attitude prizes, and the wager it makes on what lies beyond our knowledge is at times intelligent.

This is not tantamount to anything like a fully developed philosophy of religion, and neither *A Common Faith* nor any of his other writings would proffer more than an outline and a few key concepts toward such a project. It remains, however, part of a trend in twentieth-century philosophy toward articulating a spirituality that is not at odds with a scientific and secular worldview and which continues to speak of transcend ideals and of God without the cultural vestiges of bygone eras.

Notes

1 James Campbell, *Understanding John Dewey: Nature and Cooperative Intelligence* (Chicago: Open Court, 1995), 270.

2 Dewey, *Individualism, Old and New*, LW 5 (1930), 71.

3 Dewey, *Reconstruction in Philosophy*, MW 12 (1920), 106.

4 Dewey, *A Common Faith*, LW 9 (1934), 41.

5   Dewey, *Reconstruction in Philosophy*, MW 12 (1920), 89–90.

6   Dewey, *Experience and Nature*, LW 1 (1925), 43.

7   Dewey, "Education and Birth Control," LW 6 (1932), 146.

8   Dewey, *A Common Faith*, LW 9 (1934), 6, 5.

9   Dewey, *A Common Faith*, LW 9 (1934), 38.

10   Dewey, *A Common Faith*, LW 9 (1934), 17.

11   Dewey, *A Common Faith*, LW 9 (1934), 20, 28, 15.

12   Dewey, *A Common Faith*, LW 9 (1934), 23.

13   Dewey, "Religious Education as Conditioned by Modern Psychology and Pedagogy," MW 3 (1903), 215, 212.

14   Dewey, *A Common Faith*, LW 9 (1934), 8.

15   Dewey, *A Common Faith*, LW 9 (1934), 4, 9, 11, 12.

16   Dewey, *A Common Faith*, LW 9 (1934), 13, 8, 57–8.

17   Dewey, *A Common Faith*, LW 9 (1934), 25–6.

18   Dewey, *German Philosophy and Politics*, MW 8 (1915), 153.

19   Dewey, *A Common Faith*, LW 9 (1934), 14.

20   Dewey, *A Common Faith*, LW 9 (1934), 29, 29–30, 36, 35.

21   According to Robert Westbrook, "Dewey told [Sidney] Hook . . . that he had used the word 'God' because 'there are so many people who would feel bewildered if not hurt were they denied the intellectual right to use the term 'God.' They are not in the churches, they believe what I believe, they would feel a loss if they could not speak of God. Why then shouldn't I use the term?' In 1934 'God' was also a useful ally in the democratic politics of uniting the actual and the ideal to which Dewey had committed himself. 'Human beings have impulses toward affection, compassion and justice, equality and freedom,' he said. 'It remains to weld all these things together.'" Robert B. Westbrook, *John Dewey and American Democracy* (Ithaca: Cornell University Press, 1991), 427.

22   Dewey, *A Common Faith*, LW 9 (1934), 58.

23   Dewey, *A Common Faith*, LW 9 (1934), 18, 36.

24   Victor Kestenbaum, *The Grace and Severity of the Ideal: John Dewey and the Transcendent* (Chicago: University of Chicago Press, 2002), 27.

8

Aesthetics

As we saw in Chapter 7, Dewey was not averse to moving into new (to him) areas of thought at a relatively late stage in his career, and 1934's lengthy *Art as Experience* would constitute a major contribution to a field in which he had long been interested but to which he had as yet limited himself to relatively brief statements. This is one of Dewey's more difficult and sprawling works, and at approaching four hundred pages the reader may wish he had reduced its length by half, especially given the brevity of his principal statement on religion which he was composing at around the same time. Be that as it may, the book was based upon lectures he had delivered two years prior at Harvard University on the subject of aesthetics, and as would characterize so much of his philosophical work we find Dewey forswearing numerous dichotomies that have bedeviled so much of Western thought not least on the topic of art. Here again we find him resisting the kind of theoretical either-ors that this field has long presupposed and replacing these with a conception of art and aesthetic experience that is consistent with views he had long expressed on human experience in general. To understand art and the aesthetic we must begin with aesthetic experience. What mode of experience is this and what is its relation to experience's other forms? What is art itself, and in what sense is it an expression? These and some related questions would receive extensive treatment in this book, and once again my analysis in the following will endeavor to glimpse the larger picture and a few (by no means all) of the more salient details of Dewey's aesthetics.

We gain some initial insight into aesthetic experience as he would conceptualize it by means of a metaphor Dewey employed almost in passing on the first page of Chapter 1 in *Art as Experience*. "Mountain peaks," as he expressed it,

> do not float unsupported; they do not even just rest upon the earth. They *are* the earth in one of its manifest operations. It is the business of those who are concerned with the theory of the earth, geographers and geologists, to make this fact evident in its various implications. The theorist who would deal philosophically with fine art has a like task to accomplish.[1]

Aesthetic experience similarly "is" or belongs to the ordinary experience of life in a sense that he would attempt to describe in this book. It does not occur on a separate plane from life in its more ordinary manifestations but is continuous with it, as he was saying at the same time of religious experience. While "aesthetic experience" has a sufficient discreteness about it that we are able to speak of it as a distinct object of analysis, we should not imagine this as a separate department of life but as standing to the latter as a peak stands to a mountain range and as the latter itself stands to the earth more generally. What peak this is and what conceptual distinctions are possible here is what needs to be determined, and the argument begins with Dewey once again drawing attention to "the live creature" that is the human being in constant interaction with a natural and social environment.

Before turning to this theme, let us briefly note a couple of remarks he offered in the text that is the focus of this chapter and elsewhere in his work. The first is that one of the more revealing tests of any philosophy in which the concept of experience holds central stage, in his estimation, is its treatment of art and the aesthetic. Neither modern rationalism nor empiricism fared well in this regard but left us with rather anemic conceptions of the aesthetic, which leads us to question their views on experience more generally, just as his own philosophy of experience as outlined in Chapter 2 sees one of its preeminent tests in this general area of human life. Unsurprisingly, Dewey sought to develop a philosophical aesthetics that fully accords with his conception of experience in general while doing justice to the topic in its own right and while also taking into account what a range of philosophers and artists have had to say about this. Second, Dewey would periodically remark in an educational context upon the profound importance of aesthetic education, which would have surprised many of his readers given the dearth of references to this theme in his principal writings in the philosophy of education. An education in the arts is "certainly as . . . [important] as any other work done in the school," and "[i]f I do not spend a large amount of time in speaking of the music and art work, it is not because they are not considered valuable and important." Their importance from an educational standpoint is owing to their capacity to "develop the power of attention, the habit of observation and of consecutiveness, of seeing parts in relation to a whole" while also preparing us to use our leisure time throughout life for activities more edifying than entertainment or vapid amusement.[2] An aesthetic education is both instrumentally and intrinsically valuable, and if it ought not be introduced to the child at too young an age, this is not because it is an educational frill but the veritable opposite: "Just because literature is so important, it is desirable to postpone the child's introduction to printed speech until he is capable of appreciating and dealing with its genuine meaning."[3] One does not teach Shakespeare to fourth graders for the same reason one does not teach other adult subject matters prior to an age at which students are capable of grasping its meaning and appreciating its importance.

Wherein, then, lies the import and place of the aesthetic in human experience? He would speak of art as "the culminating event of nature as well as the climax of experience," but what is the meaning of this? Aesthetic experience is of cardinal importance to a well-lived life, but what "mode of experience" and indeed "event of nature" is this? The object of all experience is nature in some sense, and "[t]hings interacting in certain ways *are* experience; they are what is experienced."[4] Dewey's account would regard the aesthetic as a vital dimension of a larger experience of the world. Let us have a closer look at his analysis.

Much as and for similar reasons that Dewey opposed the spectator theory of knowledge, the notion of education as removed from extracurricular life, and any other conception of a form of experience that is disconnected from its other forms and the intelligent dimension within them, his aesthetics would directly oppose what he called "the museum conception of art" which he believed to be implicit to many an aesthetic theory at this time. The museum conception is the idea of art or aesthetic experience as a phenomenon of the gallery, concert hall, museum, or that is otherwise isolated from the regular course of experience and the settings in which it occurs. The compartmentalization of consciousness into the aesthetic, educational, religious, moral, political, scientific, and so on, and the corresponding separation of philosophical disciplines that is concerned with each is the general position against which a great deal of his thought is directed, his constant habit being to regard each of these as integrated together on a basically organic model. The leg and the arm are not one, but to speak of either as disconnected from each other or from their activity and functioning within the larger organism is a recipe for ignorance, and it is the tendency of philosophical specialists to fall into a misunderstanding of this kind. Intellectual distinctions useful within their purview commonly become inflated into stultifying oppositions, and Dewey's aim in his aesthetics is once again to conceive of art not as a separate realm but as integrated within our larger experience of life. As the mountain peak "is" the earth in one of its dimensions, art is an activity and a product that belongs to life. "When artistic objects," as he put it, "are separated from both conditions of origin and operation in experience, a wall is built around them that renders almost opaque their general significance, with which esthetic theory deals."[5]

Our temptation is to place art on a pedestal and abstract it from the ordinary business of living, and the consequences of doing so include regarding artists themselves as a race of geniuses unlike the rest of us and to idealize works of art as wholly mysterious creations. Art can assume a false appearance of otherworldliness when we focus exclusively upon objects of fine art and gallery experiences while omitting the more mundane aesthetic objects that we encounter in everyday experience and which we may not, owing to their distinction from the fine arts, even regard as artworks, from popular music to movies, photography, furniture, and so on. A philosophical aesthetics must account for all such creations and reject an elitism that would restrict our attention to Michelangelo and Beethoven. Whatever it is that makes an artwork an artwork, it is not that it participates in the same essence as whatever individual giants we care to name but something a little closer to home. For Dewey, art is continuous with community life and ordinary experience—in ways that are elusive to be sure and that require theoretical clarification, but our first step is to get out of the gallery and museum and to return to life as we experience it. Art is rooted in a culture, and if some of its finest expressions end up in spaces specially reserved for such works this should not lead us to lose sight of the ground from which they emerge. To understand art is to grasp it not in a vacuum but in relation to the conditions and activities that bring it into being. Art, he would suggest, is an activity before and more essentially than it is an object.

This basic move which Dewey and the other classical pragmatists would so often make, of calling down from the heavens what had seemed wholly celestial, arouses the ire of many an art critic of the old school as it does the philosopher of the same school. Whatever instinct it is that would have us steal away whatever it is that we prize most highly from the world in which we find it and confine it within a "peculiar and private realm" should be resisted, not because there is no separation whatever between a work of art and other kinds of objects or activities but because to grasp the nature of anything in the human world we must regard it as something living rather than a dead product. Dewey no more opposed the existence of museums, galleries, or theaters than he did schools, churches, or legislatures, but he did impress upon us an imperative against theorizing art and the experience of it in a vacuum and regarded the need of political rulers or the *nouveau riche* to display one's artistic conquests and refined taste as a base "counterpart of a holier-than-thou attitude."[6] Divorcing art from life obscures the former and impoverishes the latter. What is needed is to comprehend the two in their unity while understanding the distinctiveness of the aesthetic, and it is a task that begins by comprehending the latter in its continuity with and implicitness in experience in its other modes, again on the model of the mountain peak and the earth.

To elucidate this, let us begin with his assertion that aesthetic experience is implicit within "normal processes of living." This essentially empirical claim begins with the historical observation that from their ancient beginnings what we now classify as works of art were not "for art's sake" but

> were part of the significant life of an organized community. The collective life that was manifested in war, worship, the forum,

knew no division between what was characteristic of these places and operations, and the arts that brought color, grace, and dignity, into them. Painting and sculpture were organically one with architecture, as that was one with the social purpose that buildings served. Music and song were intimate parts of the rites and ceremonies in which the meaning of group life was consummated. Drama was a vital reenactment of the legends and history of group life. Not even in Athens can such arts be torn loose from this setting in direct experience and yet retain their significant character. Athletic sports, as well as drama, celebrated and enforced traditions of race and group, instructing the people, commemorating glories, and strengthening their civic pride.[7]

The point is more than historical, however: what would eventually be regarded as artworks having a status and a meaning distinguishable from the communal settings of which they were originally a part are never wholly severed from such contexts or from life in its more everyday connotations. The aesthetic is partially distinct from while wholly continuous with our experience of the world in general, or such is Dewey's hypothesis. To demonstrate it, he urged us to begin by reflecting not on those objects that are presented to us as works of art where the presumption is that their being such is a *fait accompli* but instead upon the nascent aesthetic quality that many an ordinary experience already contains. Consider an example from everyday life: on a summer day I notice that the lawn is in need of cutting and I proceed to gas up the machines, clear any debris from the lawn, and set to work. As I do my best not to miss any spots, to keep my lines straight, and not to run over anything that could damage the blades, after a few hours the weekly battle with nature is done and I am able to take in the general scene with a sense of satisfaction. The lawn has been transformed from shaggy to beautiful, and my appreciation likely exceeds what I would have experienced had I hired someone to do the job. It is a complete experience with a beginning, middle, and end, and where the end is not the sight of the lawn alone but a culmination of a few hours' work. The aesthetic quality of my perception arises spontaneously and quite naturally from my now completed transaction with this small corner of the earth and is neither imported into the experience from without nor in any way separate from it. The lawn does not belong in a gallery, but it does have an aesthetic quality that is one with the activity of caring for it or otherwise incorporating it into one's home.

The important things to note here are the ordinariness of the experience and its unity with the aesthetic. On Dewey's view, it is characteristic of "every normal experience" that the aesthetic is implicit within it, most often tacitly. It is not a special category of objects or faculty of mind but something that belongs in a fundamental way to the common business of living, from the relatively mundane to the more cultured and sophisticated. By a "normal experience" he meant the sort of everyday interactions with the natural and social world with which we are all well acquainted, the activities and adjustments we undertake in our daily transactions with an environment. In any such experience the aesthetic is already at work in usually nascent fashion and "is the clarified and intensified development of traits that belong to every normally complete experience." His claim is neither that all experience is aesthetic nor that art is to be identified with a given experience itself; rather, all experience is potentially aesthetic while art "is a quality that permeates an experience. . . . Esthetic experience is always more than esthetic. In it a body of matters and meanings, not in themselves esthetic, *become* esthetic as they enter into an ordered rhythmic movement toward consummation." The aesthetic quality, as he elsewhere put it, "rounds out an experience into completeness and unity as emotional."[8] The act of cutting my lawn is not inherently aesthetic, and so long as I am engaged in it, it has an incompleteness to it. It "becomes" aesthetic as it nears completion, as one can say of any action or experience that is purposeful, meaningful, or project-like. It becomes emotionally charged in the gradual achievement of unity between an animating purpose and an attained result, and it is the culmination that we properly speak of as art. "Art as experience" means not that art "is" experience but that it suffuses it under certain conditions. When we turn to the example of religious art, Dewey pointed out that throughout medieval Christendom the various arts were much the same "handmaidens of religion" that philosophy and science were, while again the notion of art for art's sake would have made no sense. The architectural design of a cathedral no less than the statuary, paintings, stained glass windows, and so on were one with the building's theological meaning. The latter objects are not doctrines but enactments of doctrine, "living experiences" in which religious ideas are animated in ways that the members of a community can more fully grasp and feel moved by in a way that is at once inward and socially shared. They enable a deepening of faith while inspiring an aesthetic appreciation which again is nothing separate and apart from the religious. "We are," in any aesthetic experience, " . . . introduced into a world beyond this world which is nevertheless the deeper reality of the world in which we live in our ordinary experiences. We are carried out beyond ourselves to find ourselves. . . . This whole" or sense of an encompassing totality that experience in general intimates "is then felt as an expansion of ourselves."[9]

The first chapter of *Art as Experience* is titled "The Live Creature," and it describes the primary mode of relationship human beings have to the world, which is dynamic, inter- or transactional, rhythmic, and purposive, order- and equilibrium-seeking, and not without what he would always call "intelligence." As biological creatures, our experience is not restricted to inner representations but is bound up with natural processes and the manifold adjustments that we make in coping with an environment which is itself vital and ever changing. Experience "signifies complete interpenetration of self and the world of objects and events" and happens as much "out there" as "in here." Classical empiricism's internal-external world opposition fails to map onto our actual experience of both the natural and social world. Our awareness is that of a live being, which like any organism negotiates its way through an environment by integrating sense and action, past and present, and various natural "rhythms" that are rooted in our biology. The "unity of experience" he described is most evident in the "live animal [which] is fully present, all there, in all of its actions: in its wary glances, its sharp sniffings, its abrupt cocking of ears. All senses are equally on the *qui vive*." The live creature's experience is a tensional and rhythmic interplay of elements and forces which develop toward a fulfillment which is "art in germ."[10] The sort of rhythms he had in mind here include the loss and regaining of equilibrium with an environment, conflict and resolution, energy and rest, tension and release, ebb and flow, seasonal repetition, disturbance and harmony, problem and solution, and myriad other instances of structured change. The world of our experience is neither disordered nor unintelligible, and if it were then aesthetic experience would not exist. It would be impossible, Dewey maintained, in a universe of flux and randomness on one hand or total completion on the other, where there is no ordered movement toward resolution, fulfillment, or satisfaction. The experience of a live being is forever on the way in one fashion or another, in constant process of realizing aims, settling conflicts, and creating harmony in a world that is sufficiently ordered to sustain this kind of experience. The unified and integrated quality of our experience is of a gradual development toward ends and a transformation of the given into what is conducive to an experience that is both enduring and fulfilling. Rhythm exists not where X merely follows Y in mechanical fashion and where the two are externally related but where a living being perceives internal relations and movement among the elements of a phenomenon, where thoughts form a train and events a narrative that is going somewhere.

Similarly, a live creature is not externally related to its world but is alive to a myriad of relations and dynamics to which it is continually adjusting itself. Its experience "like breathing is a rhythm of intakings and outgivings. Their succession is punctuated and made a rhythm by the existence of intervals, periods in which one phase is ceasing and the other is inchoate and preparing. William James aptly compared the course of a conscious experience to the alternate flights and perchings of a bird."[11] Every flight and perching, every step along the path belongs to an integrated activity where movement more closely resembles a musical movement than a teleology in which the telos lies outside of the activity and might be attained once and for all. As he would say of the activity of thinking in *Experience and Nature*, "Genuinely to think of a thing is to think of implications that are no sooner thought of than we are hurried on to *their* implications. There is no rest for the thinker, save in the *process* of thinking."[12] Every A is an anticipation of B, every B a response to A, an accommodation with C and a refusal of D, and so on and so forth in a process that ends only in death. Like James' bird, the whole thing is on the move and exhibits a unity which our intellectual distinctions have a tendency to exaggerate into wholly discrete values.

Dewey's notion of experiential culmination carries special importance here. As just noted, aesthetic experience is in principle impossible under two opposite conditions: in a world where change is utterly disordered and where it does not exist. The latter is a dead universe where all movement and activity has been played out and the whole is dissipated, while the former is one of senseless chaos. A necessary condition of the aesthetic is an experience that is changing not randomly but with intentionality and direction, where one thing follows another in the manner of any living thing. Change here does not resemble the motion of billiard balls in collision but James' bird with its rhythmic flying and settling or Dewey's activity of thinking as a step by step following of a chain of ideas. A discernible order leads the experiencer from point A to B in a fashion that is at once continuous, developmental, and heading toward an end that is not a mere stopping point but a consummation. The woodman gathering firewood engages in a variety of actions from preparing the chainsaw to clearing brush, selecting and felling trees, and splitting and stacking the wood, all in an ordered sequence that culminates in a harvest of winter fuel. Every motion of the body is oriented to this end, every lopped branch and swing of the axe a stage that draws upon what has led up to it and looks forward to the achievement of a goal that completes the activity. The entire set of actions and occurrences is held together by an anticipated purpose the eventual realization of which represents a completion. The perception of the stack of wood is not a dead cessation but an affectively charged consummation of the day's activity. The wood stack is "art in germ," not yet a work of art but an intimation of an object properly so called (a point to which we shall return).

A culmination, as Dewey would speak of it, is properly speaking a fulfillment of an ordered configuration of experience rather than a self-contained perception. It is a heightening and intensifying of what led up to it, and our everyday experience is rife with these little mountain peaks ranging from the mundane to the momentous. A conversation with a friend, reading a book, and carrying out a household chore are experiences in which we find a rhythm of particular acts which may be means toward an end or that otherwise form a unity that is comprised of stages. What matters is that there be "*a single developing activity*" where means and phases are subsumed within an integrated experience in which moments are not atoms but lead one to the next, and not only in an instrumental sense:

> In the hearing of the musical theme, the earlier stages are far from being mere means to the later; they give the mind a certain set and dispose it to anticipate later developments. So the end, the conclusion, is not a mere last thing in time; it *completes* what has gone before; it settles, so to speak, the character of the theme as a whole. In the ball game, the interest may intensify with every passing stage of the game; the last inning *finally* settles who wins and who loses, a matter which up to that time has been in suspense or doubt. In the game, the last stage is not only the last in time, but also settles the character of the entire game, and so gives meaning to all that has preceded.[13]

A completed experience may be anything from a meeting of minds to gaining an insight, reaching a book's conclusion, or a set of clean dishes in the drying rack; it need not be a life-changing event, but where it is what he calls "an experience"—or one worthy of the name—we find a progression of actions leading toward a summit.

The departure of Dewey and the other classical pragmatists from the older British empiricism must be borne in mind here. Experience remains the basis and starting point of all knowledge, but what it is not is atomistic, consisting of simple ideas or discrete deliverances of sense which come before the mind in no ordered configuration and must at some later time be cognitively arranged into coherence through the application of a method. Hobbes' mechanistic model did not map onto how we actually encounter the world and thus fails, Dewey maintained, precisely on empirical grounds. The problem with the empiricism of the seventeenth and eighteenth centuries is that it is not empirical enough and must be corrected through a more careful and phenomenological description of how the live creature engages in constant interactions that are an active "commerce with the world" rather than a mere suffering of sensations in which the mind plays no creative part. Consciousness is neither passive nor "something self-contained and self-enclosed"; indeed "mind" is better spoken of as a verb or an activity than any kind of object, one whose fundamental "animus is toward further interactions." What has happened whenever we characterize something as an experience in an emphatic sense (as in "that *was* an experience") is not that some event has merely befallen us but that we have performed an act of commerce in which some profit or loss has occurred and things are not as they were. Experience is rife with beginnings and endings, leadings and dead ends, successes and failures, again like a mountain range with its alternating peaks and valleys. The whole is not flat but is in motion, and "an experience" in a singular sense is unified by a "movement toward its close" or a leading in the direction of an ending that puts a period to a succession.[14] It is not only artists who have an eye for this, but their work does involve creating works that clarify and elevate factors in our experience that are ordinarily implicit or subdued.

Not all experiences, of course, are fulfilling or even coherent, and Dewey was hardly of the view that human life is an unending series of apogees any more than the life of the mind is a heroic disposing of every difficulty it encounters. His empirical claim is that experience generally contains a trajectory—a purpose, meaning, or destining— in virtue of which a given set of actions and occurrences hangs together in some intelligible configuration. Our actions variably succeed or fail in their intentions, but if they are without this kind of orientation, they are amorphous and unintelligible. Fragmentation exists in human life and in art, but even this may come alive to an audience through the labor of the artist or be made manifest and vivid where it had been tacit. Dewey was no sunny optimist about either art or life; experience aesthetic and otherwise includes not a little suffering, contradiction, and alienation; however, his point is not to downplay this but to draw attention to the drive in human experience toward consummations which we sometimes attain and sometimes do not. What he calls "*an* experience, in its pregnant sense"—and not all experience is so describable—"has esthetic quality" when it advances from an inception to the completion of a unified course of events and where the completion is "anticipated throughout."[15] This does not mean that we know the ending before the story is over but we sense that the game is afoot in a way that holds our attention for the duration. The characters' various doings and undergoings are not randomly arranged but are advancing somewhere in a way that is meaningful if not always beautiful or happy. The storyteller's art happens not in the midst of events but *ex post facto*; in the moment, in his example of a battle, "attention is taken up with practical details and with the strain of uncertainty. Only later do the details compose into a story and fuse into a whole of meaning. . . . [A] drama emerges with a beginning, a middle and a movement toward the climax of achievement or defeat."[16] Artistic creation happens afterwards and involves an imaginative recreating which renders explicit the completed experience and its emotionally charged fulfillment. The emotions it expresses are neither altogether discrete nor object-like but are conjoined in every instance with an experience and a situation that holds significance for us. Emotions do not stand alone but are qualities and "qualifications of a drama and they change as the drama develops"; they attend a course of events, are about them, and belong to an individual experiencer at the same time that they are had in common.[17]

A person who engages habitually and maybe professionally in artistic production is often regarded as standing at some remove from the audience who will experience their work, and the separation,

Dewey believed, is as unfortunate as the inflated distinction between the artistic and the aesthetic. The artistic is commonly thought to be the province of the artist properly so called while the aesthetic is a matter of the audience's perception, and here again the separation is overstated. It generates a false opposition between the producer and consumer of art where the former is a somewhat eccentric character if not a "genius" who in some mysterious way is unlike the person who merely consumes the products of their work. The two forms of activity are fundamentally opposed, the common view has it, and this view is a mistake. His hypothesis is that just as the aesthetic is a mode of perception that is implicit within ordinary experience, artistic creation is continuous with and emerges out of other forms of activity which we customarily regard as mundane and which are not limited to human beings. The bird constructing a nest is engaged in an activity that is proto-artistic in that it is transforming what is naturally given by integrating materials for the creation of an object that is a "satisfying culmination" of a course of activity. Moving on to the human, the auto mechanic "engaged in his job, interested in doing well and finding satisfaction in his handiwork, caring for his materials and tools with genuine affection, is artistically engaged" for the reason again that a line of activity culminates in an optimally working vehicle which may be perceived aesthetically.[18] While we are unlikely to regard the activity or the vehicle itself as an artwork, the mechanic's work anticipates or is continuous with the artistic in that the mode of activity that it involves differs mainly in the medium in which it operates. The mechanic's materials are not the musician's or the sculptor's, but in other ways we find a similar formative activity building toward an end that we see in the creation of works of art.

The mechanic's work is not likely to be seen as an act of self-expression, however, the latter notion often assumes an individualism that is both exaggerated and tangential to the form of work of which we are speaking. Artistic activity involves a good deal of expression, and in modern times the characteristic forms of expression that artists employ have been largely differentiated from its other forms, but owing less to aesthetic than to economic forces. "Because of changes in industrial conditions the artist has been pushed to one side from the main streams of active interest," creating a false severance between artistic and other kinds of expressive activity. Human expression, whether one is working in a recognized artistic medium or not, involves a transformation from some initial "impulsion"— not a raw impulse but "a movement outward and forward of the whole organism to which special impulses are auxiliary"—toward something that is more than a bodily behavior. An impulsion, which is the starting point of every human experience, is channeled into an artificial medium and thus converted into some new product. The need for rest may issue in a yawn or droopy eyelids, but these are not expressions in Dewey's sense but physical effects of a bodily state. An impulsion, need, or passion of whatever kind most often finds an outlet in a way that is relatively direct and effect-like, as joy issues in a smile or anger a clenched fist. An expression is not automatic in this way but a more imaginative transformation of an initial impulsion through a course of activity that exhibits an order which draws upon prior experiences. Artistic expression more specifically goes beyond the release of emotion to the creation of an artifact. Romantic affection may issue in anything from a smile that is not yet an expression to a love letter which may be the artistic expression that is a poem. The latter two are not simple outbursts of feeling but articulations of emotionally charged meaning in a particular medium, at once the act of articulation and the product. Thus "art is not nature, but is nature transformed by entering into new relationships where it evokes a new emotional response." Artistic production, he added, particularly when it is well executed, is not overly contrived in the sense of forcing the object of one's labor to conform to a preconceived idea or plan; instead, the artist "is taken possession of by the appropriate muse and speaks and sings as some god dictates." Like the "thinker" to whom the artist is too often contrasted, the latter does not fully control the process and does "not operate by conscious wit and will to anything like the extent popularly supposed. They, too, press forward toward some end dimly and imprecisely prefigured, groping their way as they are lured on by the identity of an aura in which their observations and reflections swim."[19] It is the theme or significance of a work of art (what it is about) rather than the creator's intention (what the artist had in mind) that appropriately guides the artist's labor and the work of the audience no less.

Dewey's claim that the division between artist and audience is conventionally overstated turns upon the kind of work that is performed by both, which is nothing as categorical as the distinction between producing and consuming. Artists do not stand to their work as pure creators ex nihilo but are "lured on" in the way just described (although he did not develop this hypothesis in detail), and by the same token audiences are not wholly uninventive recipients of another's production but have a task to perform. It is a task of affective perception, and as with more ordinary kinds of perception it is nothing as simple as a passive suffering of impressions but an active transaction with the work of art. To act and to undergo are distinct but not opposed elements of experience, and aesthetic experience is no exception. If it is evident enough that the reader of a novel or the viewer of a painting is receiving something, it is no less true that this is an active reception in the sense that it falls to them to complete what the artist has expressed, and that this completion is a recreation of the work of art itself. The latter work does not come to the perceiver as a wholly finished product—no object of experience does—but enters into the perceiver's own activity of interpretation and experience. How one responds to it is not necessarily what the artist intended, and "there is no reason why, in order to be esthetic, these experiences [of various interpreters] should be identical. So far as in each case there is an ordered movement of the matter of the experience to a fulfillment, there is a dominant esthetic quality." Not just aesthetic but all experience, for Dewey, is a joint product of the interaction of subject and object, so it would be more than odd for him to assert that an artwork's meaning is one and identical with the artist's intention. The particular consummation the artist may have experienced need not and likely will not be the same as what the perceiver experiences, as is clearly evident in the case of artworks that are culturally or historically distant from us. The Roman Colosseum or a medieval cathedral is not going to be experienced the same way that their contemporaries did, including their creators, nor may we assume they all perceived it in the same way and with the same subjective resonances that any work of art inspires. Every such work, in his words, "is recreated every time it is esthetically experienced." Additionally, it is only a work of art (an actual rather than potential one) when it is actualized in the consciousness of a perceiver. It is an unfinished universe that the live creature inhabits, and the work of art is an especially poignant example of an object that "is complete only as it works in the experience of others than the one who created it."[20]

The creation and perception of works of art are both activities in which the capacity of imagination comes to the fore. In other contexts Dewey spoke of imagination as a "dramatic rehearsal" in which one anticipates in a given line of inquiry the likely consequences of an action or hypothesis.[21] Aesthetic imagination he would define in *Art as Experience* as "a *way* of seeing and feeling things as they compose an integral whole. It is the large and generous blending of interests at the point where the mind comes in contact with the world. When old and familiar things are made new in experience, there is imagination."

The uniting factor in all imaginative activity is an integrating of whole and part, action and consequence, possibility and actuality, familiar and unfamiliar, and tradition and innovation, in a way that allows something previously unseen to become manifest. Where the unimaginative thinker may be thought of as the hyper-traditionalist who clings to the old without variation, the imaginative artist or thinker in any field is continually revising what is inherited. Indeed, "the conscious adjustment of the new and the old *is* imagination," and it is found wherever one borrows from tradition (what is received or familiar) without being a slave to it. Tradition is never a factor that can be simply dispensed of, for without it human consciousness is a blank. The content it affords is the necessary starting point of all experience, making any fundamental opposition between conservatives and anti-conservatives facile. All experiencing, thinking, and creating involves some appropriation from our forebears no less than our contemporaries, and where tradition is not an inhibiting but a living factor it is brought in contact with fresh material such that our task is one of synthesizing old and new into some novel configuration. The artist's work, then, is beholden to a tradition to which one does not stand in an abject relation but is indebted in the same manner as the "scientific inquirer, the philosopher, the technologist, [all of whom] derive their substance from the stream of culture. This dependence is an essential factor in original vision and creative expression."[22] Without giving us a fully elaborated theory of artistic creation, Dewey's aesthetics does give us an outline of what such activity consists in and its continuity with the perceiver's task, both of which are more overtly imaginative than what is implicit in more prosaic experience.

Dewey distinguished between the work of art and what he called the "*product* of art" in that the latter alone refers to an object (painting, sculpture, novel, etc., and one that is characterized by potentiality and incompleteness) while the former is best spoken of adjectivally as "a quality of doing and of what is done." Neither "art" nor "work of art" is properly speaking a noun, as the actual work of art is a working up of a given line of experience from an initial impulsion to a culmination, and where the latter is presented and perceived for its aesthetic value. The work (which is a working) of art refers to the expression (or expressing) of an affectively charged meaning, and the product in which it issues is a manifestation in intensified form of the consummatory element in experience. The product of art is the vehicle of an aesthetic perception in which is fully visible that which had been implicit in experience in inchoate form. In holding aloft some culminating moment of experience, the product "works" in and upon our own consciousness in which we actualize the potential that the product contains. Such actualization or completion is itself a complex interaction with the art product and it permits of a fair degree of relativity in how it is carried out. Unlike the product, then, the work of art "is active and experienced" where the former is "physical and potential."[23]

A final point worth noting is the role of the art critic in informing aesthetic appreciation. In Dewey's estimation, while aesthetic experience may be informed or guided by the critic, the latter's contribution can amount to a counterproductive type of judgment whereby rather than leading an audience's appreciative perception of a given work of art their activity resembles rather too closely what is practiced by the wrong kind of legal or moral judge. Too often the latter employs a standard of judgment that is fully worked out in advance and applied in doctrinaire fashion to a particular case, and a counterpart to this may be seen in a good deal of art criticism. Frequently, as Dewey put it, "[d]esire for authoritative standing leads the critic to speak as if he were the attorney for established principles having unquestionable sovereignty," for instance, in the case of the aesthetic traditionalist whose love of received forms and techniques of expression can lead them to condemn any new forms that might emerge for failing to heed values of old. Early post-impressionist painters, to mention one of his cited examples, often came in for criticism on these grounds, and the mistake of the critics here was to fail to perceive that what he called "new modes of life" and "new subject-matter" often require new forms and methods of artistic expression. The judicially minded audience or critic here fails to see that new wine must at least sometimes be poured into new bottles, and not necessarily owing to any failings with the old bottles. "[B]ecause of the relativity of technique to form, [the post-impressionists] were compelled to experiment with the development of new technical procedures. An environment that is changed physically and spiritually demands new forms of expression." The opposite error finds the critic falling into a subjectivism where aesthetic judgment is reduced to a business of "'impressionist' criticism" and personal emotionalism.[24] Aesthetic objectivism and subjectivism are likewise off base, but from this it does not follow that the art critic has no legitimate role.

The proper business of the critic as Dewey saw it is not unlike the schoolteacher or any other inquirer in that they are charged with perceiving, and showing others how to perceive, a given work in terms of its relations and meanings in context. A critic is an educator in the art of perception, and it is accomplished neither by means of fixed standards or no standards but by guiding the viewer toward what the work is expressing and by what it means. The focus properly lies not with general standards but with the particularities of a work and its "objective properties," that is, "of a painting, with its colors, lights, placings, volumes, in their relations to one another." The critique "is a survey" of the work of art in the sense that it is a description of the continuities and interrelations of its various elements which in the end may or may not issue in a judgment regarding the work's merit.

Pronouncing upon the latter is not the central business of the critic, and Dewey could be harsh in his assessment of art critics whose focus lies in playing either judge or expert rather than interpretive guide. Aesthetic appreciation crucially involves a perception which is always particularistic and inquisitive, and it is here alone that the critic has a legitimate role. In his words,

> The function of criticism is the reeducation of perception of works of art; it is an auxiliary in the process, a difficult process, of learning to see and hear. . . . The individual who has an enlarged and quickened experience is one who should make for himself his own appraisal. The way to help him is through the expansion of his own experience by the work of art to which criticism is subsidiary. The moral function of art itself is to remove prejudice, do away with the scales that keep the eye from seeing, tear away the veils due to wont and custom, perfect the power to perceive. The critic's office is to further this work, performed by the object of art.

Aesthetic experience requires a perceptive capacity where one is able to appreciatively see or hear what is being expressed, to grasp it in context, and to follow along in what one perceives. Appreciation is not a passive spectatorship but an affectively charged participation in the work itself. But to accomplish this one often needs a guide, and the critic can lead an audience to notice in a more thoroughgoing way what is happening in the work, "as a survey of a country is of help to the one who travels through it."[25] A good survey clarifies the object's various parts and the relations between them, and is properly focused not on judgments but descriptions which deepen an audience's encounter with the work.

Art or the aesthetic is no more a separate department of human experience than the religious, educational, ethical, political, scientific, or any other. The heart of his expansive philosophy is the concept of experience, and his distinctive conception of this would carry implications for so many subdisciplines of philosophy that seeing the forest through the trees has been difficult for Dewey's readers from the beginning. It remains to discuss this thinker's continuing legacy in philosophy.

Notes

1 Dewey, *Art as Experience*, LW 10 (1934), 9–10.

2 Dewey, *The School and Society*, MW 1 (1899), 64.

3 Dewey, "The Primary-Education Fetish," EW 5 (1898), 264.

4 Dewey, *Art as Experience*, LW 10 (1934), 8, 17, 12.

5 Dewey, *Art as Experience*, LW 10 (1934), 12, 9.

6 Dewey, *Art as Experience*, LW 10 (1934), 26, 15.

7 Dewey, *Art as Experience*, LW 10 (1934), 16, 13.

8 Dewey, *Art as Experience*, LW 10 (1934), 18, 53, 329, 48.

9 Dewey, *Art as Experience*, LW 10 (1934), 37, 332, 199.

10 Dewey, *Art as Experience*, LW 10 (1934), 25, 24, 25.

11 Dewey, *Art as Experience*, LW 10 (1934), 62.

12 Dewey, *Experience and Nature*, LW 1 (1925), 98.

13 Dewey, "Interest and Effort in Education," MW 7 (1913), 166–7.

14 Dewey, *Art as Experience*, LW 10 (1934), 269, 43.

15 Dewey, *Art as Experience*, LW 10 (1934), 61.

16 Dewey, *Reconstruction in Philosophy*, MW 12 (1920), 81.

17 Dewey, *Art as Experience*, LW 10 (1934), 48.

18 Dewey, *Art as Experience*, LW 10 (1934), 30, 11.

19 Dewey, *Art as Experience*, LW 10 (1934), 15, 64, 86, 79–80.

20 Dewey, *Art as Experience*, LW 10 (1934), 334, 113, 111.

21 Dewey, *Human Nature and Conduct*, MW 14 (1922), 132.

22 Dewey, *Art as Experience*, LW 10 (1934), 271, 276, 270.

23 Dewey, *Art as Experience*, LW 10 (1934), 218, 167.

24 Dewey, *Art as Experience*, LW 10 (1934), 303, 307.

25 Dewey, *Art as Experience*, LW 10 (1934), 312, 328, 313.

9
Dewey's Legacy

A thinker of Dewey's stature neither appears from nowhere nor disappears in a flash, and an appreciation of his philosophical contribution must speak briefly to both the intellectual currents that gave his thought its basic trajectory as well as the influence it has exercised in the over seven decades since his death. An exhaustive account of either topic could easily fill a few volumes; for our purposes I shall direct the reader to the bibliography, which itself is a relatively concise selection of the literature that has been published over the decades and also say a few words here about Dewey's more notable influences. From an early stage of his career, Dewey's thought can be regarded as a confluence of British empiricism, post-Hegelian idealism (the St. Louis Hegelians), Darwinian biology, liberal democracy, and an emerging American philosophical tradition, which includes elements of transcendentalism and Protestant Christianity. Dewey worked with a relatively large palette and effectively synthesized ideas from all these traditions and a good number of thinkers within each of them. The list of major influences includes G. W. F. Hegel, T. H. Green, George Sylvester Morris, James Marsh, C. S. Peirce, William James, and Charles Darwin, while lesser influences would, of course, be numerous. Whether a Locke, a Rousseau, an Emerson, or a Mill belongs on this list may be debated, but what is clear is that Dewey was appropriating ideas from these and associated figures in articulating a general outlook that encompasses the several major subdisciplines of philosophy and at the heart of which lies a theory of experimental inquiry. This theory would draw perhaps most directly and from the outset upon Hegel and James. The latter's *Pragmatism* (1907) and its sequel *The Meaning of Truth* (1909) clearly anticipate Dewey's *Reconstruction in Philosophy* (1920), *Logic: The Theory of Inquiry* (1938), and similar texts in which his experimentalism or instrumentalism would be explicitly formulated. Among pragmatists, his indebtedness is more readily apparent toward James than Peirce, although there is no denying the impact on Dewey of some Peircean notions including especially the community of inquiry, the importance of consequences, and, of course, the term pragmatism itself.

Dewey's Hegelian influence has long been underestimated in spite of his acknowledgment of the "permanent deposit in my thinking" of Hegel, which is well analyzed in James A. Good's study.[1] For a long while analytic philosophers in particular, owing either to an antipathy toward Hegel and post-Hegelian idealism or a lack of knowledge of it, regarded Dewey as having engaged in a brief, youthful flirtation with Hegel's thought only to outgrow it in his more mature work. The falsity of this was acknowledged by Dewey himself and is clearly evident to readers with more than a superficial acquaintance with Hegel and Green in particular. As late as 1945 he commented, "I jumped through Hegel, I should say, not just out of him. I took some of the hoop . . . with me, and also carried away considerable of the paper the hoop was filled with."[2] From Dewey's ontology to his politics, and at all stages of his career, the enduring influence of Hegel's dialectic, the *Bildung* tradition, and Green's organicism are unmistakable. Politically, he was America's foremost "left Hegelian" and "new liberal," although it was never Dewey's way to be a mere disciple of any of these thinkers. Employing a large palette minimizes the likelihood of discipleship, and his contributions to the various fields of philosophy were never excessively beholden to any particular influence. As he would write in a brief but important essay of 1930 titled "From Absolutism to Experimentalism" in which he spoke of his philosophical influences, "Hegel's thought . . . supplied a demand for unification that was doubtless an intense emotional craving, and yet was a hunger that only an intellectualized subject-matter could satisfy." A little further, he would add, "Were it possible for me to be a devotee of any system, I still should believe that there is greater richness and greater variety of insight in Hegel than in any other single systematic philosopher—though when I say this I exclude Plato, who still provides my favorite philosophic reading."[3] While many have noted the obvious indebtedness to older forms of British empiricism of a philosophy centered as Dewey's is around the concept of experience, his model of experience owed far more to Hegel, Green, and also Darwin than Hobbes or Hume. Experience on the latter's conception was far too atomistic and ahistorical for Dewey, while the former group offered a more dialectical and organic model of the subject-object relation which rung truer to both the youthful Dewey and in a more nuanced way to the older thinker as well.

If the story (prehistory perhaps) of Dewey's legacy begins with his own inheritance from the philosophical tradition in which he stood, it continues in the preeminence he enjoyed in Anglo-American philosophy through the first several decades of the twentieth century. Barely a major issue in English-language philosophy and American cultural life went unremarked upon by this extraordinarily prolific writer, as Dewey addressed both academic and popular audiences in a constant stream of books and essays, reviews and public talks, newspaper and magazine articles, and so on. His influence was felt not only in North America but parts of Europe and the far east, in several of which nations he had given lectures or visited at one time or another. Continental European philosophy much after Hegel and Marx interested him very little, and his somewhat unfortunate lack of knowledge of his own French and German contemporaries, including those with whom he had significant affinities, was echoed in Dewey's and the rest of the classical pragmatists' being largely ignored in European (including British) philosophical circles. In the new world, however, none gained a larger readership or exerted more influence than Dewey. By the final decade of his life, however, Dewey's influence among philosophers was being eclipsed and would remain in this condition through the next few decades. Why this came about is not owing to any devastating critique that philosophers had pronounced upon his writings but is explainable in the main by intellectual fashion. By mid-century, analytic philosophy had gained hegemony in philosophy departments throughout the English-speaking world and America's preeminent thinkers of yesteryear were beginning to go unread. Dewey, James, Peirce, and company were being replaced in the universities by the likes of Carnap, Russell, Moore, Austin, and eventually Wittgenstein and, to a lesser extent, by existential thinkers like Heidegger and Sartre. Analytic philosophy and Vienna Circle positivism had given the discipline a more rationalist bent and also a narrower and more technical orientation than what the classical pragmatists had preferred, and the latter were being relegated to the past by a new generation of academics who largely lacked more than passing familiarity with their American predecessors. As Robert Westbrook notes, "If philosophers largely ignored Dewey's work after World War II, others were even less charitable. Dewey's philosophy of education came under heavy attack in the fifties from the opponents of progressive education, who took him to task for virtually everything that was wrong with the American public school system," in spite of his limited and largely indirect influence over that system and his own critique of progressivism.[4] Such is the logic of fashion, however, and Dewey remained passé in the minds of a preponderance of philosophers from approximately the 1940s through until the 1980s.

What happened next is that Dewey's thought began to enjoy something of a resurgence—it would be overstated to call it a renaissance—which is traceable to a few factors. First, by the end of the 1960s, Southern Illinois University Press had begun to publish Dewey's complete works under the editorship of Jo Ann Boydston. The early (five volumes), middle (fifteen), and later (seventeen) works were all available by the early 1990s, and their appearance has been a boon to scholars who previously had to track down older editions and an impossible number of essays and shorter pieces from myriad locations. The complete works represent a monumental contribution to Dewey studies and to American philosophy generally, and they were supplemented in 2012 by Dewey's final and previously lost book, *Unmodern Philosophy and Modern Philosophy*, and also by his correspondence.[5] Since 1961 the Southern Illinois University at Carbondale has housed the Center for Dewey Studies which, in addition to its publishing activities, contains an abundance of scholarly resources and has accomplished a great deal to bring this thinker back into prominence. Second, by the eighties, discontent with analytic philosophy's near monopoly on American philosophy departments was on the rise and created openings for alternative approaches from classical pragmatism to various strains of continental thought. The efforts of Richard Rorty were especially important in this regard. Referring to Dewey in his popular *Philosophy and the Mirror of Nature* (1979) as one of the three preeminent philosophers of the twentieth century, along with Heidegger and Wittgenstein, Rorty effectively put Dewey back on the map for philosophers who had become disenchanted by the foundationalism and excesses of analytic philosophy.[6] Third, the secondary literature on Dewey which had never been in short supply mushroomed in the last couple of decades of the last century and has continued apace until the present. Every year an impressive number of books and articles appear that bring Dewey into contact with more current developments. The examples are far too numerous to list, but one must mention a few of the more biographical works that have shone new light upon this thinker. These include George Dykhuizen's *The Life and Mind of John Dewey* (1973) but more especially Jay Martin's *The Education of John Dewey: A Biography* (1991) and Robert B. Westbrook's *John Dewey and American Democracy* (1991). Listing some of the more noteworthy secondary works on Dewey's philosophy I shall reserve for the bibliography. Barbara Levine has compiled a multimedia CD titled *Works About John Dewey* that lists (not exhaustively) secondary works on Dewey that have appeared through 2006.

Rorty was instrumental both in reviving interest in Dewey and in inspiring a movement of neo-pragmatism which, while its relation to the thought of Peirce, James, or Dewey can be difficult to discern, has brought each of these figures back into the conversation of philosophy in often fresh and surprising ways. While Rorty's own debt to any of these three is unclear, a variety of neo-pragmatist philosophers continue to appropriate key themes from the first generation of American pragmatism and to bring all of this into contact with different currents of North American, European and even Chinese thought. Bridges with analytic and continental philosophy continue to be built by scholars in the various subdisciplines of this field. This includes political theory, where Dewey's conceptualization of democracy has lost none of its relevance. The literature of political liberalism and democratic theory has grown dramatically in recent decades, and while Dewey's name is not generally at the forefront of this, his influence remains discernible. The literature of deliberative and participatory democracy is especially indebted to this thinker, even while his name is often relegated to the background. Where practical politics is concerned, Dewey's influence has long been visible—insofar, at any rate, as a political theorist ever exercises any actual influence on real-world politics. Liberal parties and movements of recent times often take at least a page from Dewey's book, while typically discarding the rest and combining it with many a notion he would have surely opposed, as is the common fate of philosophers whose work gains some degree of popular influence. Dewey is better regarded as an ancestor—one of many—to contemporary liberal politics than a major influence. His involvement in social activist organizations such as the International League for Academic Freedom, the League for Industrial Democracy, the New York Teachers Guild, and the National Association for the Advancement of Colored People forms an additional part of his political legacy.

Finally, any discussion of this subject must include mention of the progressive education movement to which Dewey's name has been associated for over a century. As we have seen, Dewey was of (at least) two minds about a movement that claimed him as an influence while modifying his ideas quite dramatically and often beyond recognition, which prompted him to become one of this movement's most incisive and variably friendly critics by the 1930s. To this day he continues to be both credited and castigated for his influence over a movement that much like liberal democracy itself has morphed and re-morphed largely beyond anything one could recognize in Dewey's writings. Since the 1950s he has been widely blamed for the failings of public education like no other, which is a bit like blaming Marx for the Chinese Communist Party or Muhammad for the Taliban. One never knows exactly how many a "Deweyan" in political or educational circles has actually gone to the trouble of reading his texts, but such is life for the philosopher whose work gains currency outside the world of academia.

Given the resurgence of interest in this thinker that we have witnessed, it appears likely that Dewey's thought will retain a significant place in the conversation of philosophy for the foreseeable future. If a century ago he could well have been described as America's foremost philosopher, he is unlikely to regain that title, but his work does warrant a fresh look by a new generation of students and scholars working in any of the fields that we have discussed in these chapters.

Notes

1   Dewey, "From Absolutism to Experimentalism," LW 5 (1930), 154. See James A. Good, *A Search for Unity in Diversity: The 'Permanent Hegelian Deposit' in the Philosophy of John Dewey* (Lanham: Lexington, 2006).

2   Dewey, "Letter to Arthur Bentley, 1945," in *John Dewey and Arthur Bentley: A Philosophical Correspondence, 1932-1951*, ed. Sidney Ratner, Jules Altman, and James E. Wheeler (New Brunswick: Rutgers University Press, 1964), 439.

3   Dewey, "From Absolutism to Experimentalism," LW 5 (1930), 153–4.

4   Robert B. Westbrook, *John Dewey and American Democracy* (Ithaca: Cornell University Press, 1991), 542.

5   Dewey, *Unmodern Philosophy and Modern Philosophy* (Carbondale: Southern Illinois University Press, 2012). Also see *The Correspondence of John Dewey*, ed. Larry Hickman (Charlottesville: InteLex Corporation, 1999), CD-ROM.

6   Richard Rorty, *Philosophy and the Mirror of Nature* (Princeton: Princeton University Press, 1979), 5.

Bibliography

The scholarly literature on Dewey is massive. Below is a selection of books in the English language on Dewey. A much larger list of books and articles has been compiled by Barbara Levine under the title "Works about John Dewey, 1886-2016" and is available at the Center for Dewey Studies at Southern Illinois University, Carbondale.

Alexander, Thomas M. *John Dewey's Theory of Art, Experience and Nature: The Horizons of Feeling*. Albany: State University of New York Press, 1987.

Anderson, Charles W. *Pragmatic Liberalism*. Chicago: University of Chicago Press, 1990.

Anderson, John. *Education and Inquiry*. Totowa: Barnes and Noble Books, 1980.

Baker, Melvin Charles. *Foundations of John Dewey's Educational Theory*. New York: King's Crown Press, 1955.

Benson, Lee, Ira Harkavy, and John Puckett. *Dewey's Dream: Universities and Democracies in an Age of Education Reform*. Philadelphia: Temple University Press, 2007.

Bernstein, Richard J. *John Dewey*. Atascadero: Ridgeview, 1966.

Biesta, Gert J. J. and Nicholas C. Burbules. *Pragmatism and Educational Research*. Lanham: Rowman and Littlefield, 2003.

Boisvert, Raymond. *Dewey's Metaphysics*. New York: Fordham University Press, 1988.

Boisvert, Raymond. *John Dewey: Rethinking Our Time*. Albany: State University of New York Press, 1998.

Boydston, Jo Ann. *John Dewey's Personal and Professional Library: A Checklist*. Carbondale: Southern Illinois University Press, 1982.

Breault, Rick and Donna Adair Breault, eds. *Experiencing Dewey*. Indianapolis: Kappa Delta Pi, 2005.

Brooke, Christopher and Elizabeth Frazer, eds. *Ideas of Education: Philosophy and Politics from Plato to Dewey*. London: Routledge, 2013.

Browne, Neil W. *The World in Which We Occur: John Dewey, Pragmatist Ecology, and American Ecological Writing in the Twentieth Century*. Tuscaloosa: University of Alabama Press, 2007.

Bruno-Jofré, Rosa and Jürgen Schriewer, eds. *The Global Reception of John Dewey's Thought*. New York: Routledge, 2012.

Bullert, Gary. *The Politics of John Dewey*. Buffalo: Prometheus Books, 1983.

Burke, Thomas. *Dewey's New Logic*. Chicago: University of Chicago Press, 1994.

Burke, Thomas, Micah Hester, and Robert Talisse, eds. *Dewey's Logical Theory*. Nashville: Vanderbilt University Press, 2002.

Camp Mayhew, Katherine and Anna Camp Edwards. *The Dewey School*. New York: Atherton, 1966.

Campbell, James. *Understanding John Dewey: Nature and Cooperative Intelligence*. Chicago: Open Court, 1995.

Carden, Stephen D. *Virtue Ethics: Dewey and MacIntyre*. London: Continuum, 2006.

Casil, Amy Sterling. *John Dewey: The Founder of American Liberalism*. New York: Rosen Publishing Group, 2006.

Chambliss, J. J. *The Influence of Plato and Aristotle on John Dewey's Philosophy*. Lampeter: Edwin Mellen Press, 1990.

Church, Robert and Sedlak, Michael. *Education in the United States: An Interpretive History*. New York: Free Press, 1976.

Cochran, Molly, ed. *The Cambridge Companion to Dewey*. Cambridge: Cambridge University Press, 2010.

Conkin, Paul. *Puritans and Pragmatists*. Bloomington: Indiana University Press, 1976.

Coughlan, Neil. *Young John Dewey*. Chicago: University of Chicago Press, 1975.

Cremin, Lawrence. *American Education: The Metropolitan Experience, 1876–1980*. New York: Harper, 1988.

Cremin, Lawrence. *Transformation of the School: Progressivism in American Education*. New York: Vintage, 1964.

Cruz, Feodor F. *John Dewey's Theory of Community*. New York: Peter Lang, 1987.

Curti, Merle. *The Social Ideas of American Educators*. Totowa: Littlefield, Adams, 1968.

Damico, Alfonse J. *Individuality and Community: The Social and Political Thought of John Dewey*. Gainesville: University Presses of Florida, 1978.

Dickstein, Morris, ed. *The Revival of Pragmatism*. Durham: Duke University Press, 1998.

Diggins, John Patrick. *The Promise of Pragmatism*. Chicago: University of Chicago Press, 1994.

Dykhuizen, George. *The Life and Mind of John Dewey*. Carbondale: Southern Illinois University Press, 1973.

Fairfield, Paul. *Education After Dewey*. London: Bloomsbury, 2009.

Fairfield, Paul, ed. *John Dewey and Continental Philosophy*. Carbondale: Southern Illinois University Press, 2010.

Fallace, Thomas D. *Dewey and the Dilemma of Race: An Intellectual History, 1895–1922*. New York: Columbia University Press, 2011.

Fesmire, Steven. *Dewey*. New York: Routledge, 2015.

Fesmire, Steven. *John Dewey and Moral Imagination*. Bloomington: Indiana University Press, 2003.

Fishman, Stephen M. and Lucille McCarthy. *John Dewey and the Challenge of Classroom Practice*. New York: Teachers College Press, 1998.

Fishman, Stephen M. and Lucille McCarthy. *John Dewey and the Philosophy and Practice of Hope*. Chicago: University of Illinois Press, 2007.

Flower, Elizabeth and Murray G. Murphey *A History of Philosophy in America*. New York: G. P. Putnam's Sons, 1977.

Fott, David. *John Dewey: America's Philosopher of Democracy*. Lanham: Rowman and Littlefield, 1998.

Frega, Roberto, ed. *Pragmatist Epistemologies*. Lanham: Lexington, 2011.

Gale, Richard M. *John Dewey's Quest for Unity: The Journey of a Promethean Mystic*. Amherst: Prometheus Books, 2010.

Garrison, Jim. *Dewey and Eros: Wisdom and Desire in the Art of Teaching*. New York: Teachers College Press, 1997.

Garrison, Jim, ed. *Reconstructing Democracy, Recontextualizing Dewey*. Albany: State University of New York Press, 2008.

Garrison, Jim, Larry Hickman, and Daisaku Ikeda. *Living as Learning: John Dewey in the 21st Century*. Cambridge: Dialogue Path Press, 2014.

Gavin, William J., ed. *In Dewey's Wake*. Albany: State University of New York Press, 2003.

Geiger, George Raymond. *John Dewey in Perspective*. New York: Oxford University Press, 1958.

Ghiloni, Aaron J. *John Dewey among the Theologians*. New York: Peter Lang, 2012.

Gilbert, James Burkhart. *John Dewey and Hull House*. Alexandria: Alexander Street Press, 2008.

Good, James A. *A Search for Unity in Diversity: The 'Permanent Hegelian Deposit' in the Philosophy of John Dewey*. Lanham: Lexington, 2006.

Gouinlock, James. *John Dewey's Philosophy of Value*. New York: Humanities Press, 1972.

Grange, Joseph. *John Dewey, Confucius, and Global Philosophy*. Albany: State University of New York Press, 2004.

Granger, David A. *John Dewey, Robert Pirsig, and the Art of Living*. New York: Palgrave Macmillan, 2006.

Green, Judith M., Stefan Neubert, and Kersten Reich, eds. *Pragmatism and Diversity: Dewey in the Context of Twentieth Century Debates*. New York: Palgrave Macmillan, 2011.

Hall, David L. and Roger T. Ames. *The Democracy of the Dead: Dewey, Confucius, and the Hope for Democracy in China*. Chicago: Open Court Publishing, 1999.

Hansen, David T., ed. *John Dewey and Our Educational Prospect: A Critical Engagement with Dewey's Democracy and Education*. Albany: State University of New York Press, 2006.

Haskins, Casey and David Seiple, eds. *Dewey Reconfigured: Essays on Deweyan Pragmatism*. Albany: State University of New York Press, 1999.

Hendley, Brian Patrick. *Dewey, Russell, Whitehead: Philosophers as Educators*. Carbondale: Southern Illinois University Press, 1986.

Hewitt, Randall. *Dewey and Power: Renewing the Democratic Faith*. Rotterdam: Sense Publishers, 2007.

Hickman, Larry A. *John Dewey's Pragmatic Technology*. Bloomington: Indiana University Press, 1990.

Hickman, Larry A., ed. *Reading Dewey: Interpretations for a Postmodern Generation*. Bloomington: Indiana University Press, 1998.

Hickman, Larry A. et al., eds. *The Continuing Relevance of John Dewey: Reflections on Aesthetics, Morality, Science, and Society*. New York: Rodopi, 2011.

Hickman, Larry A., Stefan Neubert, and Kersten Reich, eds. *John Dewey between Pragmatism and Constructivism*. New York: Fordham University Press, 2009.

Hickman, Larry A. and Giuseppe Spadafora, eds. *John Dewey's Educational Philosophy in International Perspective*. Carbondale: Southern Illinois University Press, 2009.

Hildebrand, David. *Beyond Realism and Antirealism: John Dewey and the Neopragmatists*. Nashville: Vanderbilt University Press, 2003.

Hildebrand, David. *Dewey: A Beginner's Guide*. Oxford: Oneworld Publications, 2008.

Hollinger, Robert and David Depew, eds. *Pragmatism: From Progressivism to Postmodernism*. Westport: Praeger, 1995.

Hook, Sidney. *John Dewey: An Intellectual Portrait*. Amherst: Prometheus Books, 1995.

Howlett, Charles F. *Troubled Philosopher: John Dewey and the Struggle for World Peace*. Port Washington: Kennikat Press, 1977.

Jackson, Brian and Gregory Clark, eds. *John Dewey, Rhetoric, and Democratic Practice: Trained Capacities*. Columbia: University of South Carolina Press, 2014.

Jackson, Philip W. *John Dewey and the Lessons of Art*. New Haven: Yale University Press, 1998.

Jackson, Philip W. *John Dewey and the Philosopher's Task*. New York: Teachers College Press, 2002.

Jenlink, Patrick M., ed. *Dewey's Democracy and Education Revisited*. Lanham: Rowman and Littlefield, 2009.

Johnston, James Scott. *Deweyan Inquiry: From Education Theory to Practice*. Albany: State University of New York Press, 2009.

Johnston, James Scott. *Inquiry and Education: John Dewey and the Quest for Democracy*. Albany: State University of New York Press, 2006.

Johnston, James Scott. *John Dewey's Earlier Logical Theory*. Albany: State University of New York Press, 2014.

Kadlec, Alison. *Dewey's Critical Pragmatism*. Lanham: Rowman and Littlefield, 2007.

Kestenbaum, Victor. *The Grace and Severity of the Ideal: John Dewey and the Transcendent*. Chicago: University of Chicago Press, 2002.

Kestenbaum, Victor. *The Phenomenological Sense of John Dewey*. Atlantic Highlands: Humanities Press, 1977.

Khalil, Elias L. ed. *Dewey, Pragmatism, and Economic Methodology*. London: Routledge, 2004.

Kirby, Christopher C., ed. *Dewey and the Ancients: Essays on Hellenic and Hellenistic Themes in the Philosophy of John Dewey*. London: Bloomsbury, 2014.

Kirkpatrick, Jerry. *Montessori, Dewey, and Capitalism: Educational Theory for a Free Market in Education*. Claremont: TLJ Books, 2008.

Kloppenberg, James. *Uncertain Victory: Social Democracy and Progressivism in European and American Thought, 1870–1920*. New York: Oxford University Press, 1986.

Koopman, Colin. *Pragmatism as Transition: Historicity and Hope in James, Dewey, and Rorty*. New York: Columbia University Press, 2009.

Kosnoski, Jason. *John Dewey and the Habits of Ethical Life: The Aesthetics of Political Organizing in a Liquid World*. Lanham: Lexington, 2010.

Kuklick, Bruce. *Churchmen and Philosophers: From Jonathan Edwards to John Dewey*. New Haven: Yale University Press, 1985.

Lee, Mordecai. *The Philosopher-Lobbyist: John Dewey and the People's Lobby, 1928–1940*. Albany: State University of New York Press, 2015.

Manicas, Peter W. *Rescuing Dewey: Essays in Pragmatic Naturalism*. Lanham: Rowman and Littlefield, 2008.

Margolis, Joseph, ed. *Reinventing Pragmatism: American Philosophy at the End of the Twentieth Century*. Ithaca: Cornell University Press, 2002.

Martin, Jay. *The Education of John Dewey: A Biography*. New York: Columbia University Press, 1991.

McDermid, Douglas. *The Varieties of Pragmatism: Truth, Realism, and Knowledge from James to Rorty*. London: Continuum, 2006.

McDermott, John J. *The Culture of Experience*. New York: New York University Press, 1976.

McDermott, John J. *Streams of Experience*. Amherst: University of Massachusetts Press, 1986.

McDermott, John J., ed. *The Philosophy of John Dewey*. New York: G. P. Putnam's Sons, 1973.

McDonald, Hugh P. *John Dewey and Environmental Philosophy*. Albany: State University of New York Press, 2004.

Menand, Louis, ed. *Pragmatism*. New York: Vintage Books, 1997.

Menand, Louis. *The Metaphysical Club: A Story of Ideas in America*. New York: Farrar, Straus, and Giroux, 2001.

Morales, Alfonso, ed. *Renascent Pragmatism*. Burlington: Ashgate, 2003.

Morgenbesser, S., ed. *Dewey and His Critics*. New York: The Journal of Philosophy, 1977.

Morse, Donald J. *Faith in Life: John Dewey's Early Philosophy*. New York: Fordham University Press, 2011.

Mott, Michael Seth. *Dewey's Philosophy: Applied to the Classroom*. Cincinnati: TouchSmart Publishing, 2005.

Mulvaney, Robert J. and Philip M. Zeltner, eds. *Pragmatism: Its Sources and Prospects*. Columbia: University of South Carolina Press, 1981.

Murphy, John P. *Pragmatism: From Peirce to Davidson*. Boulder: Westview Press, 1990.

Narayan, John. *John Dewey: The Global Public and Its Problems*. Manchester: Manchester University Press, 2016.

Niu, Xiaodong. *Education East and West: The Influence of Mao Zedong and John Dewey*. San Francisco: International Scholars Publications, 1994.

Novack, George. *Pragmatism versus Marxism: An Appraisal of John Dewey's Philosophy*. New York: Pathfinder Press, 1975.

Östman, Leif E. *A Pragmatist Theory of Design: The Impact of the Pragmatist Philosophy of John Dewey on Architecture and Design*. Stockholm: Royal Institute of Technology, 2005.

Pappas, Gregory Fernando. *John Dewey's Ethics: Democracy as Experience*. Bloomington: Indiana University Press, 2008.

Paringer, William Andrew. *John Dewey and the Paradox of Liberal Reform*. Albany: State University of New York Press, 1990.

Peters, Richard Stanley, ed. *John Dewey Reconsidered*. London: Routledge and Kegan Paul, 1977.

Pihlström, Sami, ed. *The Continuum Companion to Pragmatism*. London: Continuum, 2011.

Popkewitz, Thomas S., ed. *Inventing the Modern Self and John Dewey: Modernities and the Traveling of Pragmatism in Education*. New York: Palgrave Macmillan, 2005.

Popp, Jerome A. *Evolution's First Philosopher: John Dewey and the Continuity of Nature*. Albany: State University of New York Press, 2007.

Pratt, Scott L. *Native Pragmatism: Rethinking the Roots of American Philosophy*. Bloomington: Indiana University Press, 2002.

Pring, Richard. *John Dewey: A Philosopher of Education for Our Time?* London: Continuum, 2007.

Quay, John. *Education, Experience and Existence: Engaging Dewey, Peirce and Heidegger*. London: Routledge, 2013.

Quay, John and Jayson Seaman. *John Dewey and Education Outdoors: Making Sense of the 'Educational Situation' through More Than a Century of Progressive Reforms*. Rotterdam: Sense Publishers, 2013.

Rice, Daniel F. *Reinhold Niebuhr and John Dewey: An American Odyssey*. Albany: State University of New York Press, 1993.

Rockefeller, Steven C. *John Dewey: Religious Faith and Democratic Humanism*. New York: Columbia University Press, 1991.

Rogers, Melvin L. *The Undiscovered Dewey: Religion, Morality, and the Ethos of Democracy*. New York: Columbia University Press, 2009.

Rorty, Richard. *Consequences of Pragmatism*. Minneapolis: University of Minnesota Press, 1982.

Rorty, Richard. *Philosophy and the Mirror of Nature*. Princeton: Princeton University Press, 1979.

Rosenthal, Sandra B. and Patrick L. Bourgeois. *Pragmatism and Phenomenology: A Philosophic Encounter*. Amsterdam: B. R. Grüner Publishing Co., 1980.

Rud, A. G., Jim Garrison, and Lynda Stone, eds. *John Dewey at 150: Reflections for a New Century*. West Lafayette: Purdue University Press, 2009.

Ryan, Alan. *John Dewey and the High Tide of American Liberalism*. New York: W. W. Norton, 1995.

Ryan, Frank X. *Seeing Together: Mind, Matter, and the Experimental Outlook of John Dewey and Arthur F. Bentley*. Great Barrington: American Institute for Economic Research, 2011.

Sandbothe, William and Mike, eds. *The Pragmatic Turn in Philosophy*. Albany: State University of New York Press, 2004.

Savage, Daniel M. *John Dewey's Liberalism: Individual, Community, and Self-Development*. Carbondale: Southern Illinois University Press, 2002.

Schilpp, Paul Arthur, ed. *The Philosophy of John Dewey*. Evanston: Northwestern University Press, 1939.

Seigfried, Charlene Haddock, ed. *Feminist Interpretations of John Dewey.*
    University Park: Pennsylvania State University Press, 2002.

Shaker, Paul. *John Dewey and the Knowledge Base for the Beginning Teacher.*
    Washington: Pergamon Press, 1990.

Shook, John R. *Dewey's Empirical Theory of Knowledge and Reality.* Nashville:
    Vanderbilt University Press, 2000.

Shook, John R. *Dewey's Social Philosophy: Democracy as Education.* New York:
    Palgrave Macmillan, 2014.

Shook, John R. and Paul Kurtz, eds. *Dewey's Enduring Impact: Essays on
    America's Philosopher.* Amherst: Prometheus, 2011.

Shook, John R. and Joseph Margolis, eds. *A Companion to Pragmatism.* Malden:
    Blackwell, 2006.

Shuford, Alexandra L. *Feminist Epistemology and American Pragmatism: Dewey
    and Quine.* London: Continuum, 2010.

Silva, Fernando M. Soares. *John Dewey and Karl Jaspers: Main Philosophic
    Concepts and Educational Implications.* San Rafael: Ecos Lusiadas
    Publications, 1998.

Simpson, Douglas. *John Dewey.* New York: Peter Lang, 2006.

Simpson, Douglas, Michael Jackson, and Judy Aycock, eds. *John Dewey and the
    Art of Teaching.* Thousand Oaks: Sage Publications, 2005.

Sleeper, R. W. *The Necessity of Pragmatism: John Dewey's Conception of
    Philosophy.* New Haven: Yale University Press, 1986.

Smith, John E. *Purpose and Thought: The Meaning of Pragmatism.* New Haven:
    Yale University Press, 1978.

Soneson, Jerome Paul. *Pragmatism and Pluralism: John Dewey's Significance for
    Theology.* Minneapolis: Fortress Press, 1993.

Stroud, Scott R. *John Dewey and the Artful Life: Pragmatism, Aesthetics, and
    Morality.* University Park: Pennsylvania State University Press, 2011.

Talisse, Robert B. *A Pragmatist Philosophy of Democracy.* New York: Routledge,
    2007.

Talisse, Robert B. *On Dewey: The Reconstruction of Philosophy.* Belmont:
    Wadsworth, 2000.

Tan, Sor-Hoon. *Confucian Democracy: A Deweyan Reconstruction.* Albany:
    State University of New York Press, 2003.

Thayer, H. S. *Meaning and Action: A Critical History of Pragmatism.*
    Indianapolis: Hackett, 1981.

Tiles, J. E. *Dewey.* London: Routledge, 1988.

Tilman, Rick. *Thorstein Veblen, John Dewey, C. Wright Mills and the Generic
    Ends of Life.* Lanham: Rowman and Littlefield, 2004.

Wang, Jessica Ching-Sze. *John Dewey in China.* Albany: State University of New
    York Press, 2007.

Weber, Eric Thomas. *Rawls, Dewey and Constructivism*. New York: Continuum, 2010.

Welchman, Jennifer. *Dewey's Ethical Thought*. Ithaca: Cornell University Press, 1995.

West, Cornel. *The American Evasion of Philosophy: A Genealogy of Pragmatism*. Madison: University of Wisconsin Press, 1989.

Westbrook, Robert B. *John Dewey and American Democracy*. Ithaca: Cornell University Press, 1991.

White, Morton. *Origins of Dewey's Instrumentalism*. New York: Columbia University Press, 1943.

Index